Openings in History

Series Editor: Robert Unwin

Prehistoric and Roman Britain

Alan Jamieson

Hutchinson of London

Hutchinson & Co. (Publishers) Ltd
3 Fitzroy Square, London W1P 6JD

London Melbourne Sydney Auckland
Wellington Johannesburg and agencies
throughout the world

First published 1979
© Alan Jamieson 1979

Drawings © Hutchinson & Co. (Publishers) Ltd 1979

Set in IBM Univers and Century by Tek-Art Ltd

Printed in Great Britain by The Anchor Press Ltd
and bound by Wm Brendon & Son Ltd,
both of Tiptree, Essex

British Library Cataloguing in Publication Data

Openings in history: Prehistoric and Roman Britain.
   1. Great Britain — History — Juvenile literature
   I. Jamieson, Alan
941   DA32

ISBN 0 09 136551 1

Contents

1 How do we know?

1 Identify the main features of the hill fort by matching the numbers on the photograph with the descriptions.

Number	Feature
	the ditch that surrounded the fort
	the earth banks on either side of the ditch
	the main entrance to the fort
	the place where huts once stood
	the approach road

2 Write a brief description of each pot in the picture.

3 Draw a larger version of one of the pots. Make sure that you copy the markings carefully.

4 Look at the shape of each pot. What might it have been used for in the Bronze Age?

An air photograph of a hill fort at Uffington in Oxfordshire

A set of pots and a mace-head, now in Lincoln Museum, dating from the Bronze Age

The study of the past

The history of Britain in ancient times has to be pieced together from scraps of information and by slow, careful detective work. *Archaeologists* are people who dig with a spade and trowel to find evidence of how people lived in the past. Gradually they put together the bits of information and scraps of evidence to build up a record of what actually happened.

Digging for history

There are various kinds of *evidence* and information used by archaeologists:

1 *The soil* Layers of soil pile up over time, so by digging down they find different periods of remains, with the oldest at the bottom.

2 *Wood* Scraps of wood and charcoal sometimes lie in the holes where the wooden posts of a building once stood. Wood also colours the soil around it.

3 *Stone* The placing of stones, the inscriptions (writing) on them, the carved figures of gods, men and women — all tell us a lot about forts, towns, walls, camps and houses.

4 *Metal* From metal objects we know about weapons, tools, kitchen utensils and jewellery.

5 *Pottery* In the rubbish heaps of ancient

5 On the stone, can you find three letters for the Roman word for 'Emperor' (*Imperator*)?

6 What letters are used for 'Legion' and for the number of the legion (it was the 2nd)?

7 Which of these three emperors was responsible for building the Wall (the stone has his name): Tiberius, Claudius, Hadrian?

8 Suetonius was the general in command of the Roman army at the crossing of the Menai Straits to Anglesey. How can you tell that this account was written by a Roman?

9 Draw a plan to show how the soldiers crossed the Straits.

10 Why were the Romans afraid? Write a personal account as if by a soldier in the Roman infantry, showing his feelings as he attacked.

11 Describe the same scene from the point of view of the Britons, who were being invaded by unknown foreigners.

12 Write out a list of the kinds of evidence that archaeologists and historians use in working out what happened in the past.

A stone from the wall built by the Romans in north Britain

'Flat-bottomed boats were built to carry the infantry across. The cavalry made their way over by a ford. In deeper water they swam beside their horses. A dense mass of armed men lined the opposite bank. In and out of their ranks ran women dressed in black, with loose hair, and carrying flaming torches. Behind them stood the Druids, lifting their hands high, and shrieking awful curses. This weird sight paralysed our men . . . .

'Suetonius shouted, telling them not to be afraid of a pack of women. Our men advanced, cut down everyone they met, and drove the enemy into their own altar fires.'

An extract from a book by Tacitus, a Roman writer, who in the Annals of Imperial Rome *(written about AD 100) described an attack by the Roman army on the island of Anglesey, in North Wales*

---

towns and houses are scraps of pottery (and sometimes whole pots) which, because of their different markings and shapes, tell us about industry, home life and their date.

6 *Bones* They provide information about animals killed and eaten, and about the humans who ate these animals.

7 *Coins* They can be dated. They also show that people traded with each other.

8 *Air photographs* In recent years photographs of fields, taken from an aeroplane, can show by the different heights of the crop that there may be foundations of buildings lying beneath the surface.

The writers

This is not the whole story. Sometimes (as for the Romans in Britain) there are writers who have left descriptions of life 2000 years ago. Julius Caesar, the Roman general who led the attacks on Britain in 55 and 54 BC, wrote his own history. Another writer, Tacitus, described the campaigns of the army in north Britain. These writers sometimes gave a very one-sided view of events if they did not think much of the enemy. For instance, some Romans considered the Britons to be ignorant barbarians.

2 Apes and men

1 Did the tyrannosaurus live on flesh or plants? What helps you to decide?

2 Find pictures of other dinosaurs in reference books, library books or in *A Book of Dinosaurs* by T. McGowen. Compare the size of their legs, their skins and scales and their heads. Which do you think would survive most easily?

3 Draw a time chart to scale, placing dinosaurs, Southern Ape-man, Erect man and Neanderthal man against their correct dates.

4 Write a description of the development of flint tools, including how they were made and how they were used.

An artist's drawing of a tyrannosaurus

The dinosaurs

Over a period of millions of years the earth gradually cooled. In the seas and rivers the earliest forms of life developed. These were tiny fishlike creatures that could move, feed and breathe.

As the level of the seas fell, some fish crawled on to land and became *amphibians*, able to live on land and in the water. Later, as the earth dried and cooled, the *reptiles* ruled the land. For 140 million years the greatest of all reptiles were the huge, scaly *dinosaurs*.

Then 65 million years ago the dinosaurs died out, but the *mammals* survived. Among those mammals were apes, from which developed man.

Ape-men and cavemen

The first ape-men to roam the earth were about 4 feet tall (just over 1 metre). They could walk on two legs, and so they could pick up pebbles and sticks to use as tools. They are known to us as the *Southern Ape-men*. They hunted animals (such as mammoths, wolves and reindeer) for food, and collected seeds and fruit.

As Southern Ape-men became more skilful, their bodies changed. From skulls and skeletons, we know that they had low foreheads, a ridge over their eyes, broad flat noses, and brains which were twice the size of the earlier ape-men. They made tools from hard stones such as *flint*.

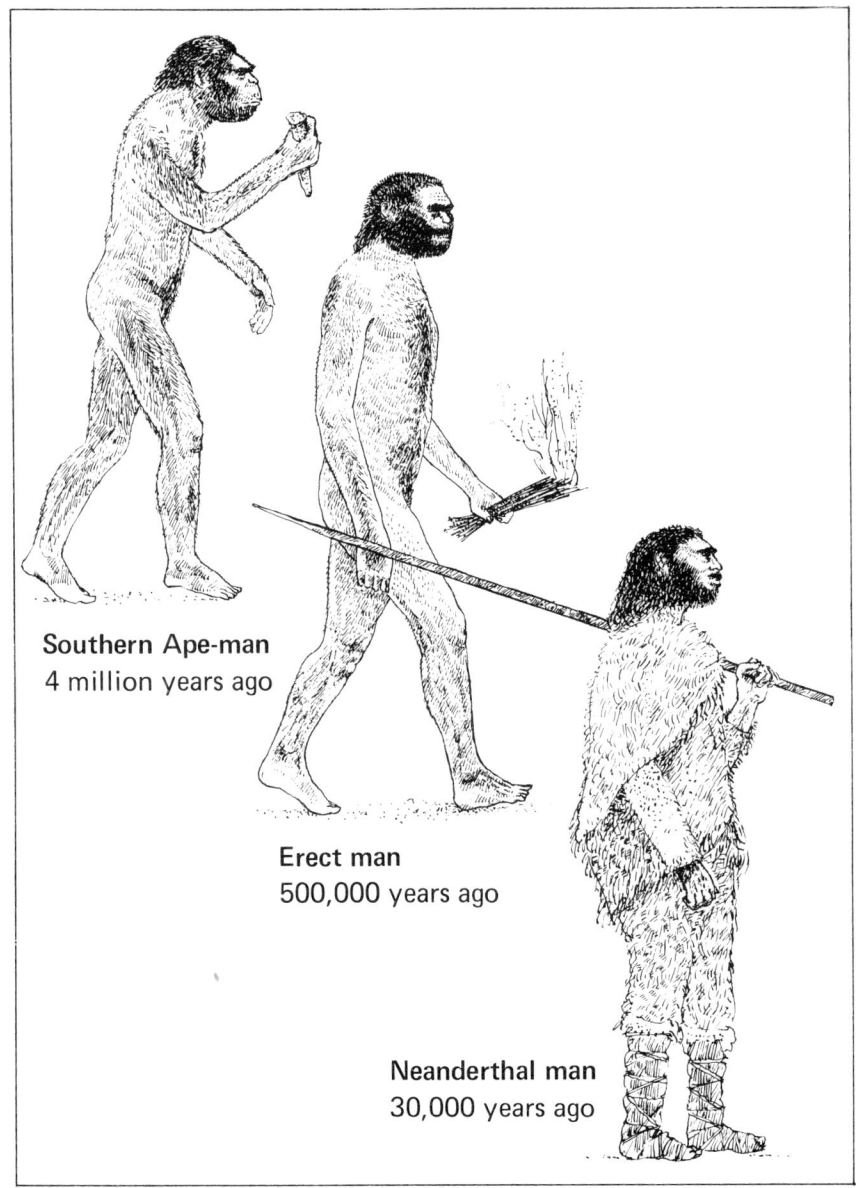

Southern Ape-man
4 million years ago

Erect man
500,000 years ago

Neanderthal man
30,000 years ago

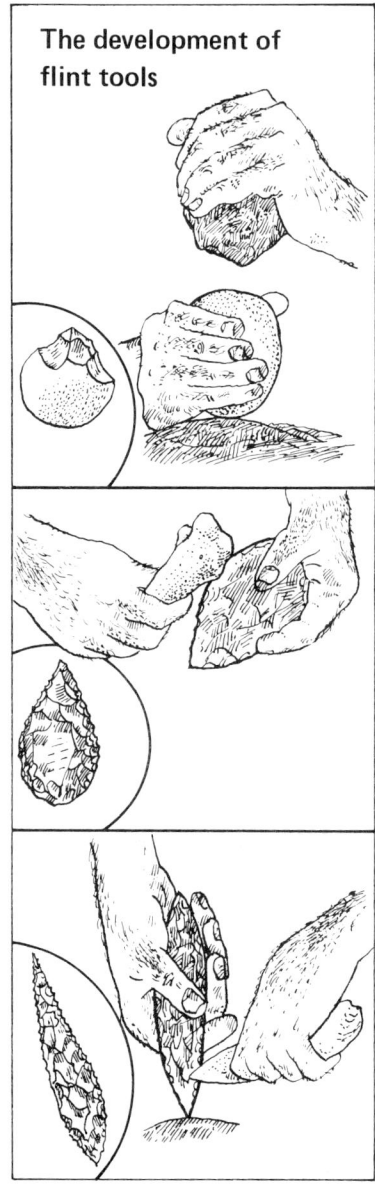

The development of flint tools

They hunted the larger animals, like elephants. They also cooked meals over fires. A man of this type is now called *Erect man* (because he stood more upright than the ape-men) by archaeologists.

A later group of men, called *Neanderthal men* (named after a place in Germany where their bones were found), started hunting in the forests. They sometimes buried their dead in graves, together with stone tools and weapons. This shows that at least some of these cavemen hunters may have thought about life after death.

Man was developing slowly all this time. From the size of cavemen's skulls, it has been found that the part of the brain that could think and remember grew larger. In the next stage of man's development, *Cromagnon man*, the growing use of tools shows us that these men had learned how to think and communicate.

Over a period of thousands of years, the hunters had become more skilful at making tools to help them survive. Their first tools were simply pebbles, with a few large flakes knocked off with another pebble to make a cutting edge. The hand axe was more efficient. It was made sharper by knocking off smaller flakes with a piece of wood, bone or later, even finer tools.

By this stage, Cromagnon man had reached the same physical development as modern man.

3 The Stone Age

The picture is an artist's idea of a forest camp beside a lake. The picture is based on an excavation at Star Carr in Yorkshire. The settlement dates from about 10,000 years ago

1 What are each of the people doing?

2 What are their houses made of?

3 What tools and weapons are they using?

4 Find pictures of tools and weapons used in the Stone Age, and draw examples to show how they developed over many years.

Into the Stone Age

The whole period when stone tools were used, from 5 million years BC to 2000 BC, is called the Stone Age. It was broken by Ice Ages, when glacial sheets covered much of Europe.

By the time of Cromagnon Man, men and women were living in natural caves in the hillsides. They hunted wild animals for food, by driving animals that could run fast over the edge of a cliff, or by capturing them in traps hollowed out from the ground.

We can tell from the stone weapons and tools that have been found that they were cleverer than earlier men. At first they used hard stones such as pebbles and flint for their knives, chisels, scrapers and axes. Later on, thousands of years later, they made tools from new materials, such as animal bone, the tusks of mammoths and the antlers of reindeer. They skinned the animals to make clothes (sewn with needles made of bone); they built shelters of animal skins, supported by wooden poles and held down with stones; and they cooked food over fires. As time passed, new weapons were made. A long harpoon or spear was used to hunt reindeer and to spear fish, and bows and arrows were invented. They learned how to tie sharpened stones to wooden handles to make hammers and axes.

5 Stone Age men admired the bison because of its strength. Where does the strength lie in the animal in the picture?

6 Draw a picture of Stone Age men and women at work on a wall painting in a cave with their brushes and dyes.

7 The horse was not a domestic animal for Stone Age men. It was hunted for only one reason. What would that be?

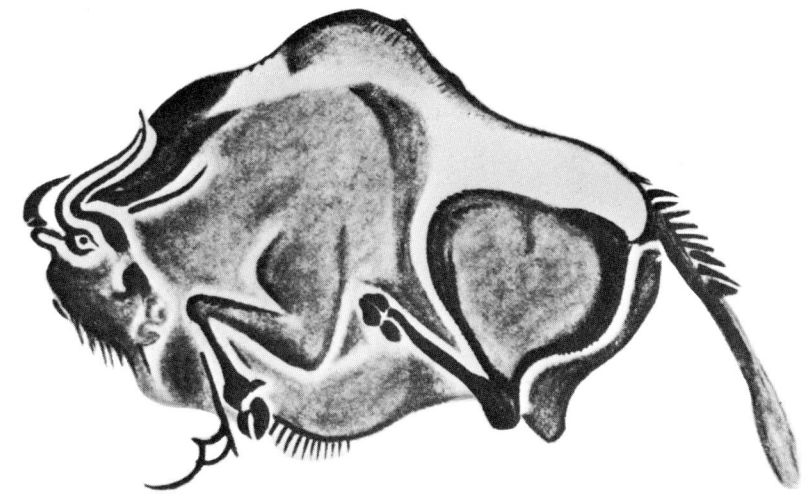

A wall painting of a bison in a cave at Altamira in Spain. It is thought to have been painted about 10,000 years ago

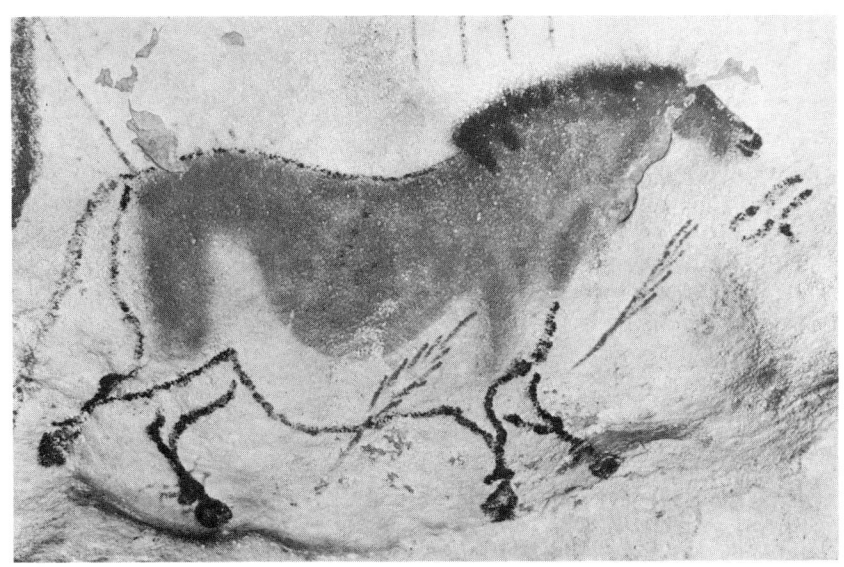

A wall painting of a horse in a cave at Lascaux in France, believed to have been done about 20,000 years ago

By 7000 BC they had learned how to use dogs in their hunting, and how to strengthen their buildings by sinking wooden posts into the ground and by adding turf to the roof.

In the lands of the Middle East, along the rivers Tigris and Euphrates, there were farming villages by 7000 BC (that is, 7000 years before the birth of Christ). But in Britain the farming of the New Stone Age did not come until around 3500 BC.

Cave paintings
In France and Spain, but not in Britain, caves with wall and ceiling paintings from the Stone Age have been discovered. Pictures of cattle, reindeer, mammoths and other animals have been found: these are all animals hunted by the cavemen.

The colours in the pictures are yellow, red, orange and black. Brushes were made by chewing the ends of plants. Plants and other dyes were used to make the paint. Why were these pictures made? No one knows for sure. Sometimes the pictures show arrows sticking into the sides of the bulls. Were the pictures drawn to bring success to the hunter? Were they part of their religion; did man believe the drawings had magical powers, or were they only for decoration?

4 Farms and villages

*Inside the burial mound
at West Kennett, Wiltshire*

1 Describe or draw a plan of the mound.
How many separate rooms, opening off the
passageway, can you see?

2 The dead were buried in the side rooms.
How do you think the different rooms were
used?

3 Stone Age men buried tools and weapons
with the bodies. Write out a list of items
from this page that they might have buried.

4 Write out the numbers 1
to 6. Link the numbers
with these descriptions:
a perforated head for a mace
a cooking pot
arrowheads
a drinking cup
a battle-axe head
a polished stone axe-head

5 What do you think Stone
Age men and women
used each item for?

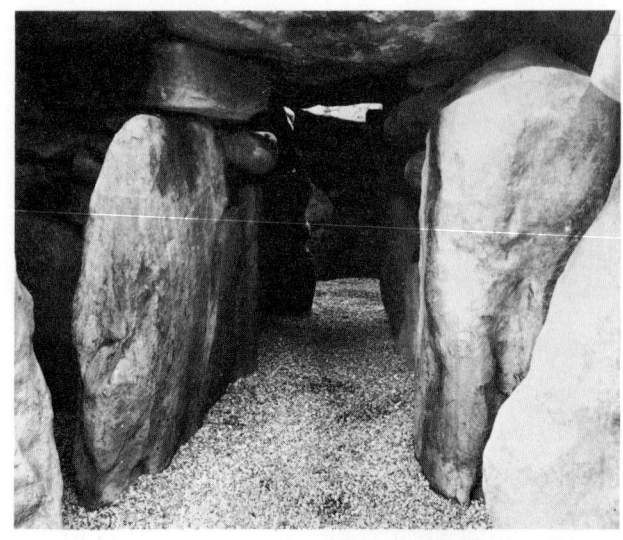

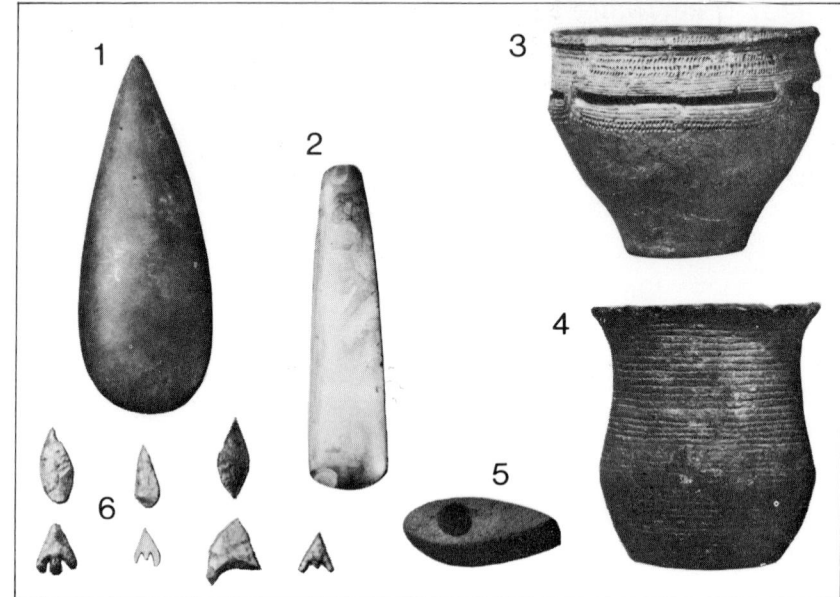

The first farmers

Britain did not actually become an island until about 6000 BC. It was later, around the year 3000 BC, that the first invaders came to Britain. They probably crossed the Channel in small boats, carrying cargoes of cattle, sheep and seed-corn. They would have found a land covered by thick forests. On the chalk and limestone hills of southern Britain they cleared the trees and sowed wheat and barley on small plots of land. Cattle, pigs, goats and sheep were kept, and wooden shelters were built for their families and animals.

As time passed, the skills of Stone Age men improved. The period when men began to farm as well as hunt is known to us as the *New Stone Age*. They used the same materials for tools and weapons — stone and flint — but they learned how to grind axe-heads and daggers, and to flake arrow-heads into sharp edges. They made pots from clay, and used these pots to collect milk from cattle and sheep. Pots were also used for cooking.

The men and women of the New Stone Age believed that after death the spirits of the dead lived on. So they buried the dead in large graves, along with food, clothes, tools and weapons for the next world.

The inside of a hut at Skara Brae, in the Orkney Islands of Scotland

6   Where was the fire in this Skara Brae hut? How would the smoke escape?

7   Find the wall-cupboards which were used to hold food, tools and weapons.

8   Draw a plan of the Skara Brae hut. Show the position of the fire, the cupboards, and the bed (which was covered with heather and bracken).

9   Draw a picture of the village as it would have been at the time the Stone Age people lived there. (The village had seven huts; their roofs were made of turf, the rafters of whale-bone, and the walls of stone.)

Burial mounds

The New Stone Age farmers buried their dead in long mounds of earth called barrows. These mounds varied in length from 25 metres to over 100 metres. Inside the barrows were burial chambers, sometimes made of stone blocks. A passageway allowed people to enter or leave the mound. The barrows are likely in some cases to have been the family vaults of chiefs of the local tribe. Long barrows can be found in Ireland, Wales, Scotland and southern Britain.

The villages

The huts and villages of the farmers of the New Stone Age have long since disappeared because they were built of wood, turf and animal skins. But at Skara Brae, pictured above, a village of seven little huts has been found. The island always had very few trees but plenty of stone, so the village was built of stone huts. When the villagers left, the site was covered with sand, which preserved it for thousands of years.

People entered the one-room houses by creeping through a low door cut in the thick wall. The door was a slab of stone, held in place by a whale-bone bar.

5 Stonehenge

Above: *Stonehenge is a monument of stones on Salisbury Plain, in Wiltshire. The picture, taken from the air, shows the pattern of stones. There was an outer ring of thirty upright stones, set deeply into the ground. On top of them was a continuous circle of flat stones called* lintels. *These outer stones were all called* sarsens

1 How many lintels can you see in their original positions? (The lintels were curved and angled so that they sat on top of the upright stones.)

2 Inside the outer circle were groups of three stones called *trilithons*. How many trilithons can you see? How many do you think there were originally?

3 What were *bluestones*? (The text below will help you.) In the picture, work out where the bluestones were placed.

4 Use library books (or the Department of the Environment guidebook to Stonehenge) to find a picture of Stonehenge as it was when complete. Draw a picture of it then.

Little is known about the people who set up the great circles of stone at Stonehenge. Archaeologists think that it was begun about 2000 BC, and that there were three different building periods.

Sun and moon worshippers
In the Stone Age, men and women worshipped the sun and moon, and believed that spirits lived in the trees and hills. They built circles of stone to worship these gods. One theory about Stonehenge is that people travelled to it to worship the sun. The stones are arranged so that they point exactly in the direction of the sun on midsummer's day.

The first people at Stonehenge dug a ditch to surround the site. The earth from the ditch was banked up and inside it men dug fifty-six holes. No one knows what the holes were for, but later on they were used to bury human bones. Then work stopped and the second stage of building did not begin until about 200 years later.

The second group of people to come to Stonehenge transported eighty stones (each 1.5 metres high), called *bluestones* (the granite has a bluish tinge), from Wales. The bluestones were brought by sea, up the River Avon and then dragged over land. The stones were set up in a wide outer circle.

The upright stone has a stone knob at the top. When the lintel was raised, the hole fitted over the knob to make a neat joint

5 Using the scale, work out the approximate height (to the nearest metre) from ground level to the top of the knob.

6 Can you find a bluestone in the picture? Using the sketch-map, describe where the stones came from. By means of a drawing or diagram, show how the bluestones were brought by sledge and boat to Stonehenge.

Diagrams to show how a lintel was raised into position

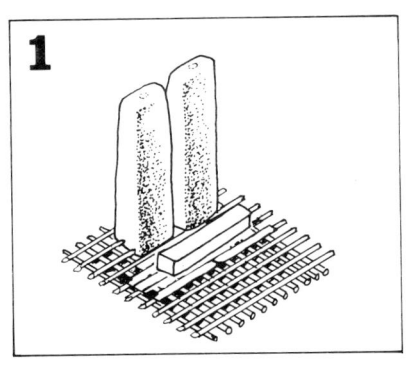  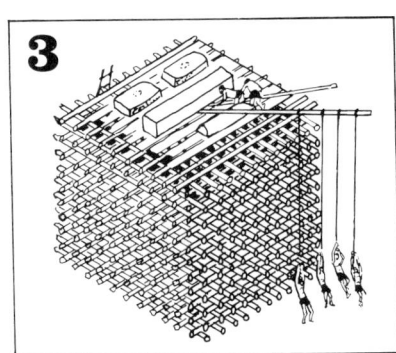

In the third stage of building the great stone temple was built. About 20 miles away were huge stones lying on the hillsides. They were dragged to Stonehenge on sledges. To pull a stone over a hilltop probably needed over one thousand men. The stones were chipped and smoothed with stone axes and hammers and were set up in position. Inside the circle of uprights and their lintels were the five trilithons. Some of the old bluestones were placed in a ring inside the temple.

How the stone was brought to Stonehenge

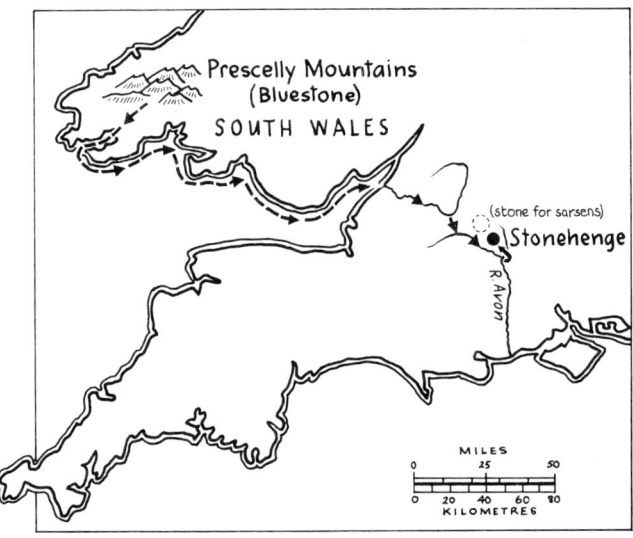

6 Bronze Age burials

Silbury Hill is the largest historical man-made mound in the whole of Europe. There have been many excavations of the hill in the past, and in 1970 another thorough investigation was made

1   The base of Silbury Hill covers an area of 2 hectares (about 5 acres). The width of the road on the far side of the hill is about 12 metres. How many metres high do you think the hill is: 10, 40, or 100?

The Beaker Folk

About 2000 BC, invaders crossed the Channel from the mainland of Europe. They are known as the Beaker Folk because archaeologists have found beaker-shaped pots that were used by them. The Beaker Folk were the first to use metal. They had copper axes, knives and daggers, and ear-rings and brooches of gold.

Copper is a soft metal, and smiths (people who worked with metal) discovered that if copper is added to a little tin, a much stronger metal, bronze, can be made. Tools and weapons (such as swords, shields and axes) had been used in the lands of the Middle East about 3500 BC, and it is

possible that the Beaker Folk learned about bronze from travellers. The Bronze Age came to Britain gradually and much later, about 2000 BC.

Armed with new weapons, the chieftains of Wales, Cornwall, Ireland and southern England formed strong tribes. They fought each other, and traded their tin and bronze with people on the mainland of Europe. They exchanged their goods for precious gems such as amber and gold rings. They buried their treasures with their chiefs in round barrows. Many of these barrows can still be seen in the countryside of Britain today.

Bronze Age warriors liked drinking and feasting. This open cauldron would have hung by chains over an open fire

The bronze trumpet might have been used to call the warriors to battle

Below: *The artist's drawing shows the circles of stone at Avebury as they may have stood thousands of years ago*

2   What use might the ring on the cauldron have had?

3   Draw a picture of a warrior blowing the trumpet.

4   On the picture of Avebury, match these parts of the temple to the numbers:
the bank and ditch
the outer circle
the inner two circles
the main entrance
Why do you think Avebury was built?

5   How do you think the chieftains of the Bronze Age became wealthy men, even though they were only simple farmers?

The great stone circles

In the Bronze Age there were, of course, no proper roads. Thick forests covered the valleys. But people had to move about. The travellers therefore kept to the hilltops and walked or rode along rough tracks called ridgeways. These tracks can still be seen (and are still used) on the chalk and limestone hills and downs of southern England.

At this time the great stone circles were built at Avebury and Stonehenge on the open spaces of Salisbury Plain. At Avebury, the stone temple was so large that a village now stands inside it. There was a great circle of stones, some weighing up to 40 tons. Inside it were two smaller circles. Outside the whole area was a circular bank and ditch. How these great stones were raised is still a mystery. The Avebury stones were dragged only a few miles, unlike the bluestones of Stonehenge which came from Wales.

In the same part of England archaeologists have found very fine bronze and gold objects. They belong to a warrior people who lived after the Beaker Folk. In other parts of Britain were many different tribes. Some buried the ashes of their dead in urns, sometimes under burial mounds called barrows.

7 The Celts of the Iron Age

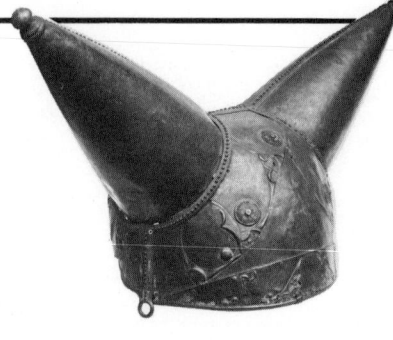

Right: *A bronze helmet, found in the Thames near London. It may have belonged to a chief*

This bronze facing once covered a chief's shield, made of wood or leather which therefore rotted away. The bronze is studded with red glass and enamel

1 Draw a picture of a Celtic warrior chief, wearing this helmet and carrying this shield. (The drawing of the Celtic chief in Opening 8 will help you with the rest of his clothing.)

2 What evidence is there in these pictures to show that the Celts were an artistic people?

3 Make a list of the objects mentioned in this Opening that Celtic women would use:
for their daily work
for their hair and clothing

4 Where did the Celts come from? What differences would their knowledge and use of iron make to their way of life?

This bronze mirror was found at Desborough in Northamptonshire. On the back of the mirror is an intricate design

Carved bone combs like this one were used in the weaving of woollen cloth

The new iron weapons

From about 800 BC, Britain was invaded by groups of people called the Celts. They came from Gaul (modern France and Belgium) and seized control of the south-east of Britain. In place of bronze, the Celts found out how to use a harder, tougher metal, iron, to fashion into tools and weapons.

Until the Romans came to Britain much later and wrote about the Celts, there was almost nothing written about them. As with the people of the Stone Age and Bronze Age, we have to rely on archaeological evidence. Excavations and air photographs tell us about their settlements and their way of life.

Archaeologists have found out how the Celts protected their villages and families from attack. They have also dug up rings, mirrors, bracelets and other personal ornaments; weapons and armour; bowls and pots, and farming and household tools.

From all this evidence we know that the Celts lived together in family groups which eventually became large tribes. They had chiefs to rule over them. The chiefs lived in the biggest huts in the village. The tribes often went to war with each

A reconstruction of an Iron Age farm at Little Woodbury, near Salisbury

5 Part of the harvest is drying on the racks and poles. What crops can you find?

6 What animals did the Celts have?

7 How was the farm protected?

other, so they built wooden stockades around their isolated farmsteads. In time of war they gathered together on a hilltop, protecting themselves with ditches and earth banks.

The Celts also used an early kind of wheel. The first one was made of wood. Later they learned how to make spokes, so that carts and wagons were able to move more quickly. Using wheels, the Celts then made the chariots that gave their armies the speed and mobility which surprised the Romans. The Celts were skilful people. They decorated everyday articles such as brooches, rings, mirrors, combs and bracelets with intricate designs. A chief's weapons such as his sword, shield and helmet often had gems or glass embedded in them, as you can see above. As well as bronze and iron, the Celts used gold, silver, jet and amber for decoration.

Metal workers became very skilful at fitting glass, bone and precious stones into very small objects. From the jewels that have been found, we now know that the Celts were an artistic as well as a warlike people.

8 The Celts at war

Above: *The early chariots had solid wooden wheels. This is an artist's idea of a chariot used around the year 200 BC*

Below: *A model of a later chariot from the National Museum of Wales*

A Roman coin used at the time of the Roman invasion of Celtic Britain. By this time the chariot had reached its final stage. It was a light cart, pulled by two ponies

1 What differences and improvements can you see in the development of the chariot?

2 How had the chariot been made lighter?

3 What changes can you see in the development of the wheels?

4 According to Julius Caesar, how did the Celts use their chariots in battle?

The chariots

When the Romans came to Britain, they were surprised by the fighting powers of the Celtic tribes. The Romans were able to defeat the Celts because the tribes did not join together in a single large army. The Romans were able to deal with the tribes one by one, picking off each one in turn.

The Romans were very impressed by the Celtic use of the war chariots. These gave the Celtic soldiers an opportunity to dash about a battlefield, leaping from the chariots to fight with sword or spear, and then to move to another place.

This is what Julius Caesar, the Roman general in the invasion of 55 BC, wrote about the charioteers in his book, *The Conquest of Gaul*:

In chariot fighting the Britons begin by driving all over the field, hurling their spears. The terror caused by the horses and the noise are enough to throw their enemies into disorder.

Caesar also admired the control of the driver in the two-man chariot (one man drove the chariot, the second was the warrior):

Even on a steep slope they are able to control the horses at full gallop and turn them in a

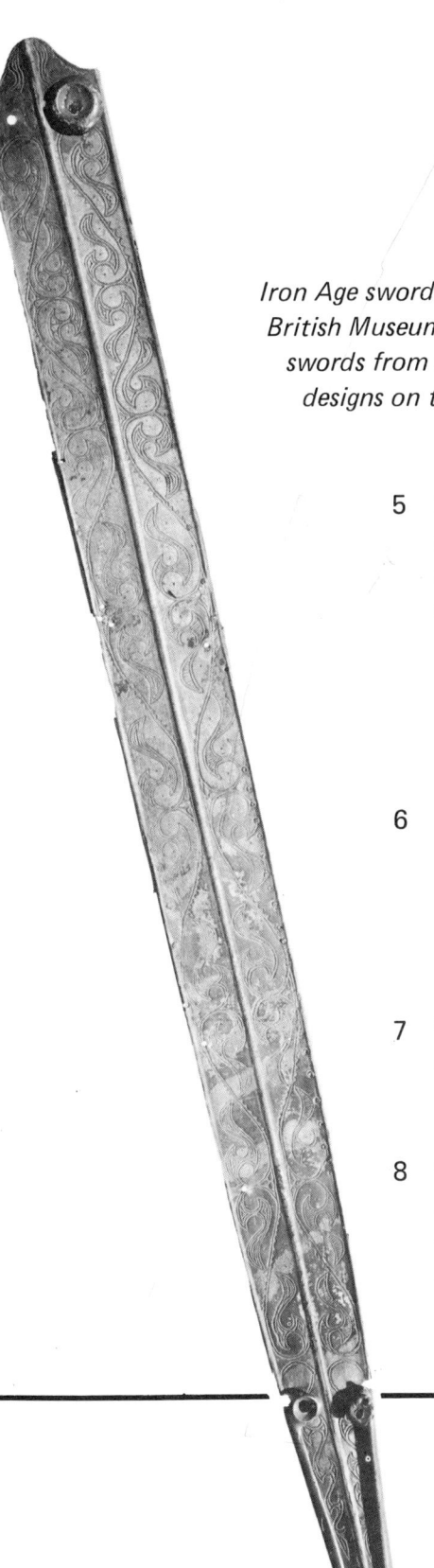

Iron Age sword of the Celts (now in the British Museum). The Celts made their swords from iron, with finely worked designs on the scabbards

5 Write down these periods of history in the correct order in which they occurred:
   Iron Age
   New Stone Age
   Bronze Age
   Invasions by the Romans

6 About how many years passed between the completion of Stonehenge and the first invasion of the Romans?

7 What kind of designs can you see on the sword? Draw some of them.

8 What effects, according to Julius Caesar, did the Celtic chariots have on their enemies?

Time chart	
5000/ 4000 BC onwards	**New Stone Age** farming, plants and animals flint and polished stone tools and weapons pottery long barrows
2500 BC onwards	Beaker folk Stonehenge begun round barrows
2000 BC onwards	**Bronze Age** bronze tools Stonehenge finished
1000 BC	**Iron Age** hill forts, as at Maiden Castle Belgae invade
55 BC	Julius Caesar invades Britain
AD 43	Conquest of Britain by Romans begins

moment. They can run along the chariot pole, stand on the yoke, and return to the chariot as quick as lightning.

The Celtic warriors

Any insult or threat to a Celtic tribe was followed by an attack. They raided each other's lands for cattle and plunder. Sometimes, when two tribes faced each other, one warrior would step forward to challenge a chief from the opposing army. This fight to the death either settled the dispute or was followed by a general battle.

A Celtic chief must have been a very impressive man. His bronze helmet would glint in the sunlight. In his hand he would grasp an iron sword, with a dagger at his belt and a spear held ready for fighting at long range.

9 Hill forts and brochs

The hill fort at Maiden Castle, in Dorset, seen from the air. The hill fort is thought to have been the capital of the local tribe. It covers a large area of 45 acres in all

1   For protection, the Celts dug ditches around the fort and piled the earth into banks or ramparts. How many earth banks and ditches can you find surrounding the hill fort?

2   What buildings might there have been at the centre of the fort?

3   At each end of the hill fort, the entrance was hidden by a maze of ditches. Can you find a way through the maze?

Hilltop forts

Many Celts lived in lonely farms such as the one at Little Woodbury (See Opening 7). Other families lived in hilltop villages, heavily protected against enemy tribes. The outlines of the defences of these forts can be seen in photographs taken from the air. The first of these hill forts usually had only a single circular ditch and an earth bank, but later forts such as the one at Maiden Castle often had several rings of ditches and earth banks. You can therefore see from the rings how the sites of the forts have been developed.

An enemy force, after crossing the earth banks and ditches, would then come face to face with a wooden fence. Inside it there would be huts for the Celtic families, and a pen for the sheep and cattle.

The huts were cone-shaped, as at Little Woodbury, with a roof of turf or thatch. In the one-roomed hut a fire would burn in the central hearth, with the smoke escaping from a hole in the roof.

For furniture, the Celts probably had wooden bunks and beds, a simple table and a stool or two. They covered the bed with animal hides.

For cooking, the village people used pots and pans, and a big cauldron to boil meat.

4   Make a list of the differences in the geo-graphical features (land, sea, position, etc.) of Maiden Castle compared with the Mousa broch.

5   What differences can you see in the fortifications of the two places?

6   Are there any weak points at Mousa or Maiden Castle? If you were leading an attack, how would you try to break in to both places? (Use diagrams or sketch-maps to illustrate your answer.)

7   Find the Shetland Islands and Mousa on a map. Where would the raiders come from to attack Mousa? (You will need to look at a map of northern Europe to work out the answer.)

Above: *A broch or fort on Mousa, one of the Shetland Islands of Scotland*
Below: *A cross-section of a broch*

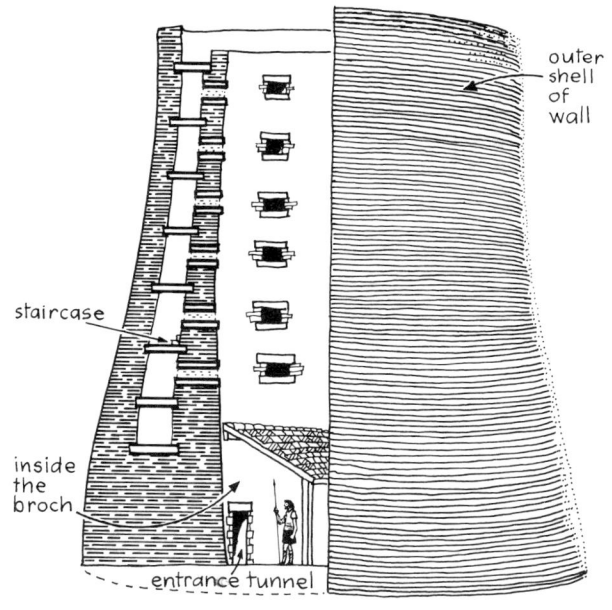

outer shell of wall

staircase

inside the broch

entrance tunnel

The brochs

The people who lived in the far north of Celtic Britain built a different kind of castle or fort. To protect their farms and lands from attackers, the Celts who lived in what is now northern Scotland built high towers called *brochs*, or walled forts called *duns*.

The brochs were most unusual and striking buildings. They were tall, windowless towers, over 12 metres in height. The walls were made of two layers of stone with a hollow space in between. Within this space were staircases and small rooms. At the centre of the broch was a courtyard usually about 12 metres across. In this area the families could live until raiders had gone. Most of the brochs were built beside the sea. They not only gave protection to the farmers and their families from sea rovers, but they also provided good look-out posts to spot approaching ships.

The weakest part of the broch would be the entrance. The Celts therefore cut a very narrow entrance through the thick stone, so that people had to crawl in to reach the centre. During a raid, the people inside would feel quite safe, even though attackers might fling arrows and stones, or try to set fire to the broch.

10 Britain before the Romans

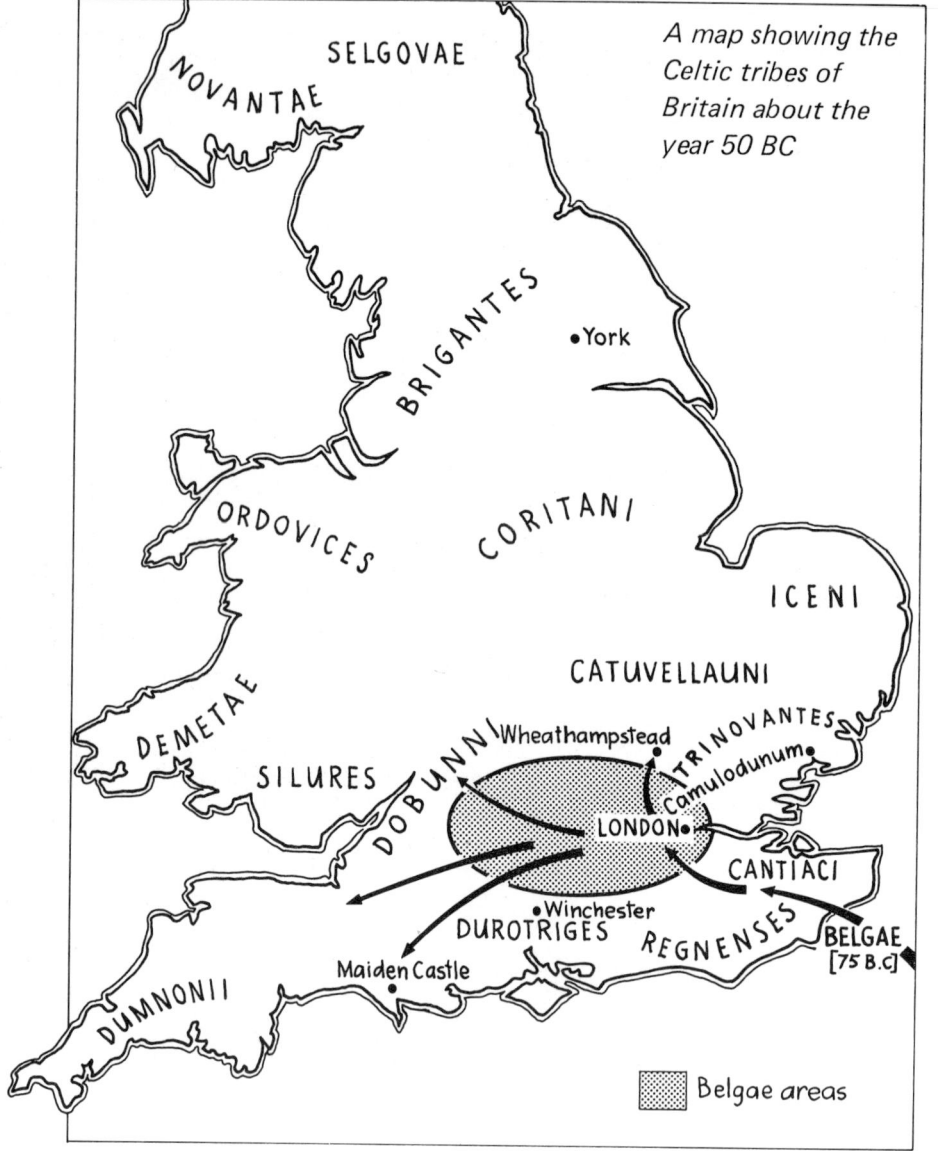

A map showing the Celtic tribes of Britain about the year 50 BC

Belgae areas

Coins from Celtic Britain, minted at Colchester

1 Which letters on the coins are abbreviations for the ruler, Cunobelinus, and the 'capital' township of Camulodunum?

2 From these coins, what would you say were two of the main commodities for trade?

3 Copy or trace the map of the Celtic tribes into your notebook. Mark in colour all the areas occupied by the Belgae.

The invaders from Europe

In about the year 120 BC, another group of invaders came to Britain. They were also Celts, called the Belgae, whose name still survives in modern Belgium. The Belgae were a warlike people, who used horses and chariots in battle. They settled in the region of the Thames valley, pushing other Celtic tribes to the north and west. In 55 BC came another invasion, the Roman invasion of Julius Caesar. But the Romans returned to Gaul soon afterwards, and the Belgae were able to start their attacks on other tribes again. Over a long period of nearly one hundred years they established firm control over southern Britain. The tribal hill forts were sacked and destroyed or else were occupied by the Belgae. They built their own 'capitals', that is, settlements protected by earth-banks or ditches. These were constructed at Wheathampstead, Camulodunum (Colchester) and other places.

The Belgae traded with other tribes both in Britain and on the mainland of Europe, and with the Romans. Some Roman items have been found in the remains of Belgic houses — jewellery, coins, tools and pottery. In exchange, the Belgae sold corn, cattle and metals. The leaders of most of the tribes, like Cunobelinus (AD 10-40), issued their own gold coins.

Julius Caesar, in The Conquest of Gaul, *wrote:*

'There are only two classes of men who matter at all. The common people are treated like slaves, never do anything without being told to, and are never asked for their opinions . . . . The Druids take charge of the worship, act as judges in almost all arguments, and do not have to fight or pay taxes. The warriors go into battle with their servants and dependants.'

Diodorus Siculus, a Greek, wrote:

'The men as well as the women wear bracelets on their wrists and arms, and thick rings of gold around their necks. They wear finger rings and even golden tunics. They have striped cloaks fastened with buckles . . . . They are terrifying to look at with deep-sounding voices. And they are boasters and threateners, and yet they are quick-witted and learn fast.'

4 How many main groups or classes in Celtic Britain did Julius Caesar write about? List what each class of people did.

5 In what ways were the Belgae different from the other Celtic tribes? Write down three or more ways in which they changed Britain.

The ditch surrounding the township at Wheathampstead in Hertfordshire

The Celts worshipped many gods and goddesses who were believed to have their homes in rivers and woods. The priests were the Druids who made animal sacrifices to the gods.

By the time that the Romans conquered Britain (from AD 43 onwards), most of southern Britain had fallen into Belgic hands. In other parts of the country, older tribes such as the Iceni of Norfolk and the Brigantes of Yorkshire had their own kingdoms. When the Romans did come, the fiercest resistance to them came from the Belgae. When the Belgae were finally defeated, the Iceni and other tribes gave in quickly to the new rulers. The people of Britain in the first century AD were thus no longer savages painting their skins with woad. They were well organized in large kingdoms as successful traders and farmers, and they produced fine jewellery and other articles which are still admired today for their craftsmanship.

11 Caesar invades Britain

A statue of Julius Caesar, now in Rome

Julius Caesar, the commander of the Roman army which invaded Britain, wrote an account of the invasion in The Conquest of Gaul. *As the Roman ships neared the coast of Britain, Caesar saw the British tribesmen lining the beach:*

'He [Caesar] ordered the warships (which were swifter and easier to handle than the transports) to be rowed hard and run ashore. From this position the slings, bows and artillery could be used by men on deck to drive back the natives. As the Romans still hesitated, the man who carried the eagle of the 10th Legion cried out in a loud voice, 'Jump, unless you want to surrender our eagle to the enemy.' At this, the soldiers leaped out of their ships, and as soon as they had got their footing on the beach, they charged the enemy and put them to flight.'

1 Examine the pictures of Julius Caesar and the Roman warship carefully. Then draw a picture showing the Romans landing on the beach.

2 In the picture of Julius Caesar, what armour is he wearing? What kind of shoes does he have? What extra clothing would he need if he was about to lead his troops into battle?

3 In your own words, describe how Caesar very cleverly used the warships to bring all his troops into battle.

In search of fame

The first Roman invaders to land in Britain were led by Julius Caesar. In the year 55 BC Caesar was a general in command of the armies in Gaul (modern France). He decided to sail across the narrow seas and invade Britain and win a great victory. A triumph such as this would make the Roman people sit up and take notice! Traders had told him that Britain was rich in gold, cattle and corn, and that the Britons had been supplying his enemies in Gaul with food and weapons. His plan was to defeat the Britons and return to Gaul with his ships full of corn and gold. However, the Romans found that the British tribesmen

fought fiercely. A sudden storm wrecked some of Caesar's ships, and a legion sent to look for corn was attacked and suffered heavy losses. Caesar went back to Gaul, saying it had been a successful raid and that he intended to return.

In the following year he took a bigger army of 2000 cavalry (horsemen) and five legions — about 20,000 troops altogether. On this second invasion there were no British tribesmen waiting on the beaches. He landed without any difficulty and marched inland. The first battle was fought several miles from the sea. Although the British tribes fought bravely, rushing at the legions with their swords and spears, the discipline and training

The stone carving from a monument in Rome shows soldiers on board a Roman warship

4 How many oars are there in this galley (a ship rowed by oars)?

5 From the way that the men are dressed, would you say they are soldiers or sailors?

6 The Romans needed to protect themselves. What do you think the wooden turret in the centre of the ship was used for?

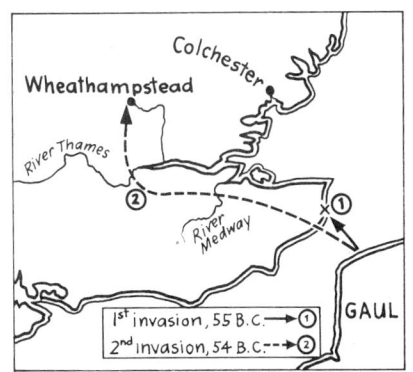

The map shows the two invasions of Britain by Julius Caesar

7 Find the routes followed by Caesar in 55 BC and in 54 BC. Why did he aim for Wheathampstead in the second invasion? (See the text below.)

8 Can you think of another route that Caesar might have used to reach Wheathampstead? Why, do you think, did he not use an easier route?

9 Using the *Oxford Junior Encyclopaedia* or other reference books in the library, describe what happened to Julius Caesar after he left Britain. Write an account of what he did and how he died.

---

of the Romans gave them the victory. Caesar led his troops across the rivers Medway and Thames (see the map) and marched towards the great camp of the Britons at Wheathampstead which was surrounded by deep ditches and banks of earth. Caesar defeated the tribesmen and entered the town in triumph. The local chiefs then surrendered to the Romans and signed a treaty, promising to pay tribute to the Romans, probably in the form of coins. Caesar was now ready to return to Gaul and so he and the army marched south, embarked on the ships and sailed away. Caesar won many other battles and eventually became the ruler of all the Roman territories.

But he never again returned to Britain.

After the Romans had left, a new king, Cunobelinus, ruled in southern Britain. He moved his main camp to Colchester. In the years between 54 BC and AD 43 the Britons traded with the Romans in Gaul, but no more legions (for the time being) crossed the narrow seas to disturb them.

12 The conquest

The picture shows a bolt fired from a ballista *(a Roman catapult on wheels) locked into the spine of a British tribesman. Archaeologists who excavated the banks of earth at Maiden Castle in Dorset found a skeleton with the bolt still in it*

1   What part of this bolt or arrow is missing? What would be the effect on a tribesman of being hit by this bolt?

2   Trace or draw the map of southern Britain into your book, with the lines of advance of the four legions. Four places are marked on the map as Lo, L, M.C. and Co. Write the names in full on your map. The names are all in this Opening.

3   Add the road, the Fosse Way, to your map.

4   Suppose you were a British leader such as Caratacus (see text below) advancing from Wales. By means of arrows, show how you would attack the Romans.

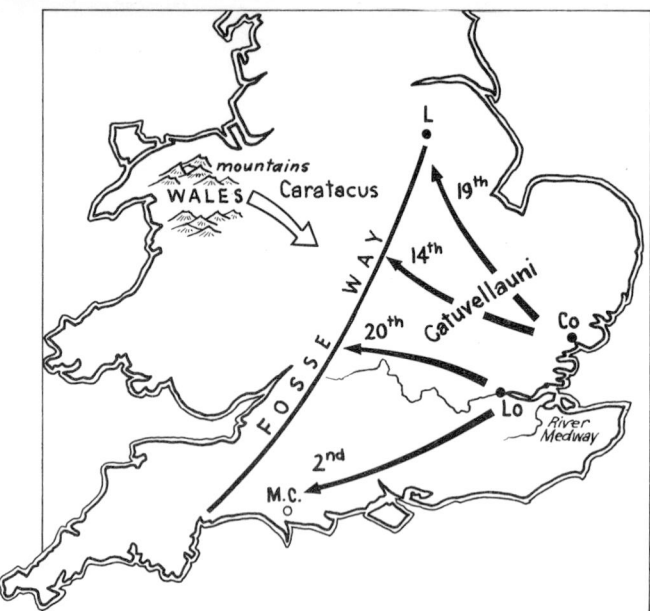

The Romans try again

Over ninety years after the invasion by Caesar's army, another fleet left Gaul. Emperor Claudius in Rome had ordered the attack. More than 40,000 men crossed the sea, landed on the beaches of southern Britain and advanced slowly to the River Medway. The two sons of Cunobelinus, who were called Togodumnus and Caratacus, decided to fight the Romans separately. This was a great mistake. Togodumnus was killed and his army fled. Caratacus was also defeated but escaped to Wales. With the leading British tribe, the Catuvellauni (see the map), defeated in battle, the other tribes gave in without a fight.

Emperor Claudius was sent for and hurried from Rome to share in the triumph. The Romans advanced towards Colchester (the Celtic name was Camulodunum, as you can see from the coins on Opening 10). After a fight they entered the defences of the town. Claudius left orders with his generals that the advance should continue after he had left for Rome.

The map shows how the four legions fanned out to attack the other tribes. According to one Roman writer, a general called Vespasian 'fought thirty battles, crushed two tribes and captured more than twenty towns as well as the Isle of

An extract from The Annals of Ancient Rome written by Tacitus, a Roman historian, about the year AD 110:

'Caratacus hurried from one place to another, saying that this was to be their day, their battle to be won. They would win freedom or be slaves for ever . . . . Every man swore that no enemy weapons and no wounds would make them give in to the Romans.

'After scouting to find the easy and difficult points, Scapula [the Roman general] led his troops forward. They crossed the river and attacked, but came off worse in wounds and men killed. However, under a roof of locked shields, the Romans demolished the clumsy stone barrier and drove the enemy to the hilltops. One group of men attacked with javelins, while the heavy infantry advanced in a tightly packed formation. The British, un-protected by helmets or breastplates, were defeated. The Romans cut them down with swords and spears. The wife and daughter of Caratacus were captured and he and his brother eventually surrendered.'

Roman soldiers attacking the wall of a town under the shelter of shields held over their heads. This stone carving is from a monument in Rome called Trajan's Column

5   Draw three strip pictures to show:
Caratacus encouraging his troops
the Romans advancing under a roof of
    shields
the hand-to-hand fighting

6   The Romans had a word, *testudo*, to describe the 'roof of shields'. The word is the name of an animal. Which of these three words do you think means *testudo*: elephant, tortoise, horse.

7   Write down three differences that you can find between the invasions of Caesar and the conquest of AD 43. (Comparing the maps in Opening 11 and this Opening will help you.)

Wight.' One of the British camps that was cap-tured was probably Maiden Castle (see the map). In the space of four years the Romans conquered the south-east corner of the country. A road called the Fosse Way was built near the boundary of the Roman zone. Within this area the legion-aries built walled camps and forts. Colchester became the main government centre with a temple dedicated to the Emperor Claudius. Londinium (London), which at first was only a collection of huts at a crossing point on the River Thames, soon grew to become a port for ships trading with Gaul and Rome.

Caratacus in chains

As the years passed, the Roman legions marched deeper into the countryside. Caratacus came out of hiding with an army made up of Welsh tribes-men. He was defeated in battle and captured. In chains, he and his family were sent to Rome but, because the Romans thought him a brave soldier, he was given a pardon.

Occasionally the tribes of southern Britain rebelled against the new rulers, but as the Romans built more roads and forts, Britons gradually accepted their Roman masters. When a new governor was appointed in AD 58, the conquest of Wales was begun by a fresh army.

13 Queen Boudicca

The tombstone of Longinus, soldier of the rank of 'duplicarius' in the Roman army. The stone was found in the cemetery of the army camp at Colchester (the Roman town of Camulodunum). The inscription tells us that Longinus died at the age of forty after fifteen years' service

1 Do you think that the bearded tribesman cowering beneath the feet of Longinus' horse was a Roman or a Briton?

2 Was Longinus in the
   cavalry (horsemen)
   infantry (footsoldiers)
   artillery (soldiers with wheeled vehicles)?

3 Write out a list of the reasons why the Iceni rebelled against the Romans.

4 The tombstone of Longinus dates from about AD 45, fifteen years before the Iceni were in revolt against the Romans. It was found at Colchester. What do you notice about Longinus' face? How do you think the tombstone came to be damaged?

The reasons for the rebellion

The Iceni were a tribe that lived in eastern Britain (see the map). After the invasion, they gave in to the Romans and for some years lived in peace. However, as time passed, the Romans annoyed the Iceni people. A large settlement of retired soldiers called a *colonia* and a temple dedicated to the Emperor Claudius were built at Colchester. The Iceni and a neighbouring tribe, the Trinovantes, were restless and so when the Roman governor went off to fight in Wales, he took all their weapons away from the Iceni, in case they rebelled.

In the year AD 60, the king of the Iceni died and his wife Boudicca became queen.

The Romans demanded that all loans of money given to the king should be repaid. When the Iceni asked for time to pay both the heavy taxes and the debts, Roman soldiers marched in and demanded money and corn. They seized the lands of the queen, and when she protested, they ill-treated her and her daughters. After this outrage the Iceni rose up in open revolt. Suetonius, the Roman governor, was in north Wales. He immediately began to march south. Each messenger brought news of fresh disasters. The Iceni had joined up with the Trinovantes and had marched

An extract from a book, The Annals of Imperial Rome, *written by a Roman historian, Tacitus, about AD 110:*

'Suetonius chose a position in a narrow valley with a wood behind him. He could be sure the enemy was not in his rear, and that the open ground to the front was free from ambush. In the centre were the legionaries; on each side of them were the auxiliaries, with the cavalry on the flanks. The bands of British infantry and cavalry were all in a mass, and wandered about the field. They were so confident that they brought their wives and set them on wagons at the rear of the battlefield . . . . Suetonius gave the signal. With careful aim the legionaries threw their javelins as the enemy came in close, and then burst forward in a wedge formation. The auxiliaries and cavalry closed in. The enemy turned tail, but escape was difficult for the wagons blocked their path . . . . Our reports said that 80,000 Britons were killed, and only 400 of our men died. Even the oxen, transfixed with spears, added to the heaps of dead.'

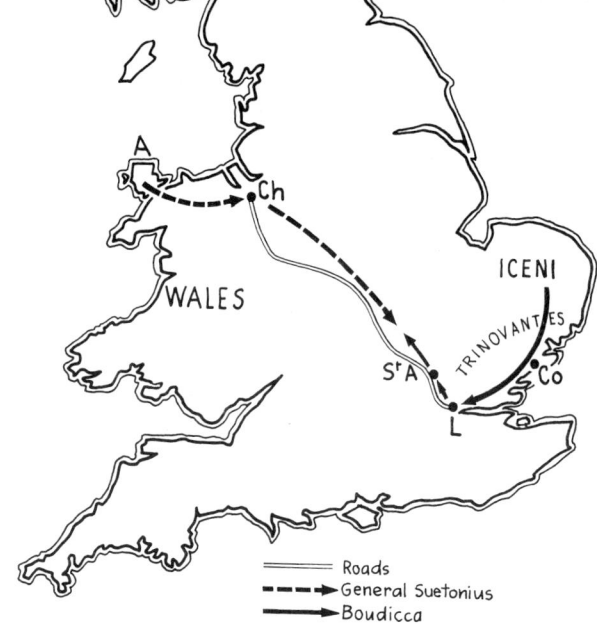

The march from Anglesey by General Suetonius and his army

5   On the map, follow the routes taken by General Suetonius and Boudicca to the battlefield. What are the names of the places shown as A, Ch, St A, L and Co? (You will find some help in the text below.)

6   What is the name of the road along Suetonius' route? (See Opening 20.)

7   Draw a plan of the battlefield described by Tacitus. Show the valley, the wood, and how Suetonius placed his troops. Add the army of Boudicca and their wagons. By means of arrows, show how the Romans won.

8   Write out some reasons to explain why and how the Romans won the battle.

---

on Colchester. The town had been attacked and the Roman veterans had all been killed. The fine new buildings, including the temple to Claudius, were burnt to the ground.

Within days, London had fallen to the Iceni. Mobs destroyed the town and murdered any Roman they found there. The town of St Albans (see the map) was next. After looting and burning it, Boudicca's army moved north.

Suetonius picked his battleground very carefully, with his back to a wood. Further north than Boudicca's forces, his troops rested and prepared for battle. They knew they had to win or be massacred.

The great battle
In the British army, food was short, people were tired and discipline was slack. Boudicca tried to rally the tribesmen: 'Let us show them that they are hares trying to rule over wolves,' she is supposed to have said. The Britons charged headlong across the battlefield. The legionaries waited and then threw their javelins as the Britons ran at them.

The tribesmen wavered, broke and fled. Queen Boudicca escaped. But she knew the Romans would pursue her and one story tells that, to avoid the disgrace of capture, she drank poison and died.

14 The Roman army

The tombstone of Marcus Favonius Facilis, centurion, was found in the cemetery at Colchester

1 Look at the inscription, which is in Latin, the language of the Romans. A legion is shown as LEG. The number of the legion follows it. Was Marcus in the 2nd (II), 9th (IX), 14th (XIV) or 20th (XX) Legion?

2 In his right hand, Marcus is carrying a vine-staff. Discipline in the Roman army was very strict. What do you think this stick was used for?

3 What kind of armour is Marcus wearing? How many weapons is he carrying? What are they?

4 Marcus was a centurion, an officer. At the time of the invasion of Britain, how many men did a centurion command?

In AD 67, Josephus, a Jewish priest, was captured by the Roman army in Israel. In a book, The Jewish War, he described the Roman army:

'They are born holding swords in their hands, and they never have a rest from training. Every day, every soldier exercises as eagerly as if he were in action. They are never paralysed with fear or exhausted by hard work. Victory is certain, for their enemies can never catch them unawares. Whenever they invade an enemy country, they never engage in battle until they have fortified a camp.'

Men and their weapons

The Roman army that conquered Britain was not large (about 40,000 men) but it was a tough and highly trained force. Of the thirty *legions* in the army, four came to Britain (the 2nd, 9th, 14th and 20th). In each legion there were 5000 to 6000 men, all Roman citizens and conscripted mainly from Italy. In every legion there were sixty *centuries*, each containing eighty men (one hundred men in the early days of Rome, reduced to eighty before the invasion of Britain). In command of the legion was a *legate*. A centurion commanded a century. Other officers were called *tribunes*.

The ordinary *legionary* carried a shield, short sword, dagger and javelin. Next to his skin he wore a vest; over this he had a tunic which reached to his knees. On his legs he wore long stockings, and on his feet he had sandals, studded with hobnails. In battle, he had body armour — metal strips stitched on to a leather jerkin covering his chest, shoulders, back and waist.

The legionary signed on for a fixed term, often as long as twenty-five years. His wages were small, and out of it he paid for food and clothing. He ate simply — usually corn made into porridge, bread, cheese, wine, or vinegar mixed with water.

The tombstone of Rufus Sita, a soldier of the 6th Thracian Cohort, was found at Gloucester. He died aged forty, after twenty-two years' service

5 Josephus gives a number of reasons to explain why the Roman armies were usually victorious. Write out these reasons in the order in which you think them most important.

6 What weapons is Rufus Sita carrying?

7 Was Rufus a foot-soldier, an archer or a cavalryman?

8 What kind of animals are shown on the top of the tombstone?

9 Draw a picture of one of these three Roman soldiers:
>   a legionary
>   a centurion
>   a cavalryman

By using the pictures in the Openings, you should be able to draw an accurate picture. Below the soldier, add his Roman name (Marcus or something similar), his age, the years of his service, and his military unit — as on Rufus Sita's tombstone.

The auxiliaries and the cavalry

Only half of the Roman army were legionaries. Most of the rest were *auxiliaries*. These were soldiers who were not Roman citizens. They had been drafted into the army, and came originally from provinces of the empire: Gaul, Spain, Germany, Syria, Thrace and other lands.

The auxiliaries provided most of the cavalry. Mounted on small, sturdy horses, the cavalryman carried a sword, a long spear, dagger and shield. A quiver of short javelins was slung on the horse's flanks.

The auxiliaries were divided into *alae* and *cohorts* (not legions) of about 1000 men (500 in a cavalry cohort). There were also auxiliary infantry units (more lightly armed than the legionaries), archers, and mounted infantry (soldiers who rode quickly to any part of the battlefield, dismounted, and fought on foot). The auxiliaries usually fought on the flanks of the legions, to save the Romans from heavy casualties.

At the end of their service, legionaries received a grant of money or land. Very often, they settled down as farmers or innkeepers. After twenty-five years, auxiliaries were given the rank of a Roman citizen and some money. Many became traders; few went home.

15 Camps and fortresses

Left: *A photograph taken from the air showing a corner of the legionary fortress at Caerleon in Wales*

Below: *An artist's impression of the same corner of the fortress at Caerleon as it might have been about the year AD 200*

1 Using the photograph as a guide, draw a diagram of the fort showing the outer ditch, the outer wall, and the foundations of the corner or angle towers.

2 In Picture A there are some small circles. From the evidence of Picture B, can you say what these circles were used for?

3 In Picture B, what is the settlement beyond the walls? What were the long blockhouses inside the fortress used for?

4 Find out from a map of Roman Britain where Caerleon was. Write out some reasons to explain why you think the Romans built a fortress there.

Marching camps

During the conquest of Britain, the Romans built hundreds of fortresses, forts and camps. The remains of these forts can still be seen, particularly from the air. At the end of a day's march into unknown country, the legionaries stopped to make a camp, called a *marching camp*. They dug a ditch around all four sides, and piled the earth on the inner side to make a turf wall. If they intended staying for some time, the soldiers added a fence or row of sharpened stakes.

For the legions, the Romans built *fortresses* at Colchester, Exeter, Wroxeter, Lincoln, Gloucester, Chester, York and Caerleon. The fortresses had barracks, workshops, stables, a hospital, a jail and granaries to store corn for winter supplies.

Another kind of stronghold were the *forts*, built to control important military points such as Housesteads on Hadrian's Wall. From Richborough fort on the coast of Kent, ships sailed regularly to Gaul and to Rome.

The legionary fortresses could house almost 5000 men; the forts could take from 50 to 1000 soldiers.

A plan of the fortress at Deva Victrix (Chester)

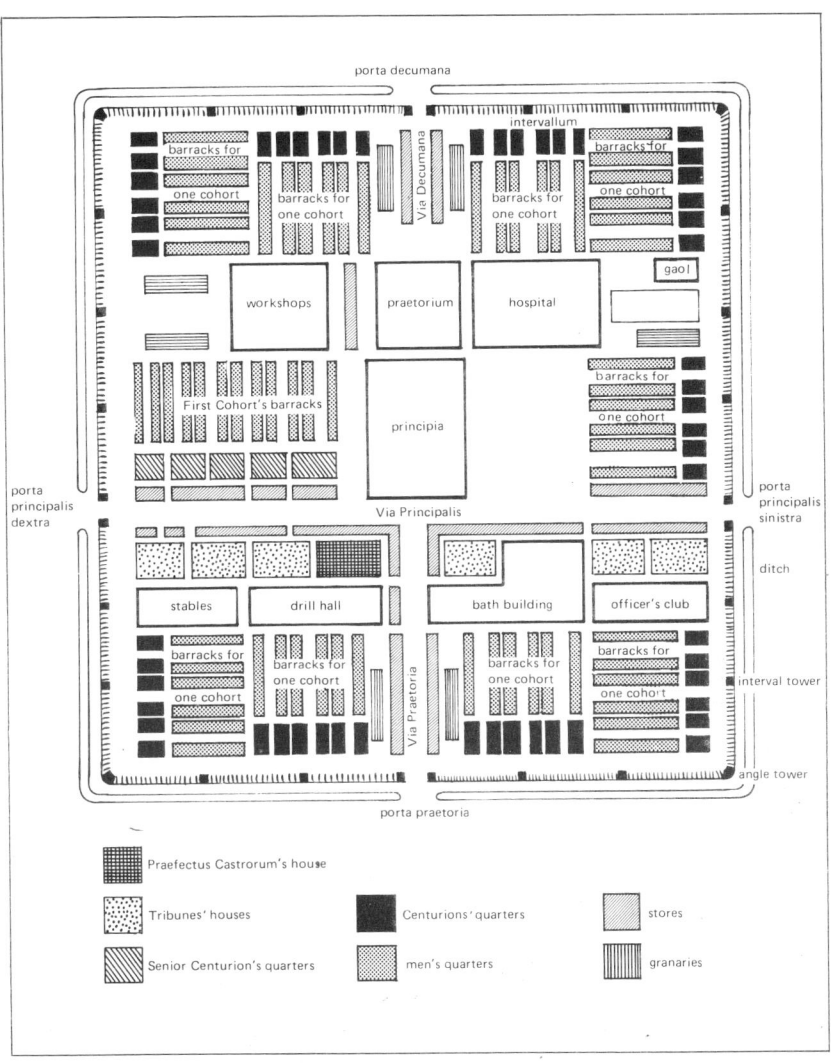

5 How many gates were there at Chester? What do you notice about their positions?

6 The *principia* was the headquarters for the garrison. Where was it placed? Why do you think it was put here?

7 Find what buildings the fort had for men who were:
   sick
   imprisoned
   officers

8 Use your imagination and draw a picture of the fort as it might have looked in Roman times. Label the different buildings.

Inside a fortress

In a fortress such as the one at Chester, the most important building was the *principia* (headquarters). In it were kept the legion's documents, records, standards, statues of gods, and pay. Nearby was the *praetorium* (the commanding officer's house), a hospital, a jail and the armoury (where weapons were kept). In long rows were barrack blocks for the legionaries, and separate buildings for officers (tribunes and centurions). Among other buildings were granaries, storehouses and stables. Crossing the fort was a main road, the *via principalis*.

Outside the walls of the fortresses were other buildings. Sometimes the main baths were outside the fort. Some of the fortresses (such as Caerleon) had an amphitheatre, a large oval building with a space (the *arena*) in the centre and seats banked up like a stadium of today. Here, soldiers trained in the use of weapons, and watched athletic contests, games and plays. The most popular contests were between men armed with swords and javelins, who were called gladiators. Also outside the walls was the village of the Britons, and the fields where corn and vegetables were grown.

16 The march to the north

This mould for a figure of a god called Taranis was made by a tribe of Caledonians, and was found in north Britain. It is thought to date from the third century AD

1   Taranis has only one weapon. What is it?

2   How was his body protected?

3   The Caledonian tribesmen of the north worshipped the gods of the hills, rivers and other parts of nature. What do you think Taranis could have been the god of?

4   Find the four main walls of Birrens fort. The main gate is on the right (1). Why do you think a line of ditches (2) was placed there?

5   Can you find any traces of buildings *inside* the fort? What buildings would they be?

A photograph, taken from the air, of the site of Birrens fort in Dumfriesshire, Scotland

The attack on Wales

After the defeat of Queen Boudicca, the Romans spent the next fifteen years recovering their hold on southern Britain. The legions marched as far north as Carlisle and York, and new roads and forts were built. The 2nd Legion moved into Wales and built a fort at Caerleon. Only one Welsh tribe, the Ordovices, was free from Roman power.

Julius Agricola came from a wealthy Roman family. He became an army officer and as a young man served in the army in the war against Boudicca. On leaving Britain he took part in campaigns in other parts of the Empire.

In the year AD 77, Agricola returned to Britain as the new Governor. He immediately moved the 20th Legion to Chester and began to squeeze the Welsh tribes. Within a year the legions had conquered north Wales and had defeated the Ordovices in a fierce battle.

From Wales, Agricola marched north. His army defeated the Brigantes tribe and marched into what is now southern Scotland. By the year AD 81 the legions had reached the River Forth, where they built a line of forts made of turf and timber. He rested for almost a year, although one patrol was sent into Galloway where they built forts such as the one at Birrens.

6 Copy the map of Britain into your notebook. From the text below, draw arrows to show *a* the line of Agricola's advance into north Wales; *b* the line of the march to Carlisle and the River Forth; *c* the march to the main battlefield.

7 Add the names of the forts shown on the map. With a dotted line draw the line of the forts in the Forth-Clyde valley. Give your map a title.

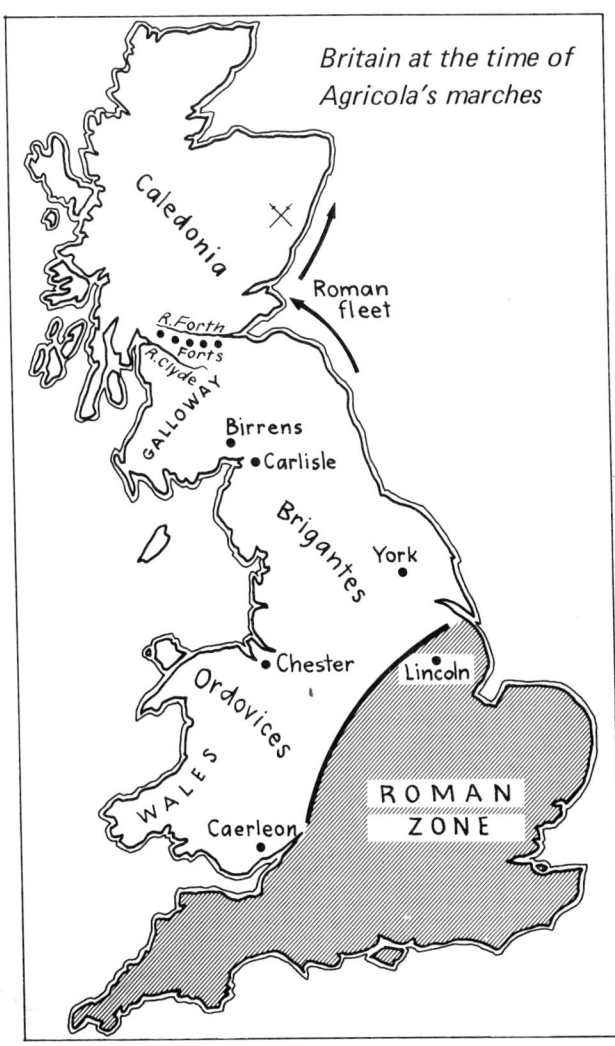

Britain at the time of Agricola's marches

Cornelius Tacitus married the daughter of Agricola. He wrote the story of Agricola's campaigns. In his book, Agricola, *Tacitus described the last great battle against the Caledonians:*

'The fighting started with both sides throwing spears. The Britons showed their skill in stopping the spears with their swords and shields. Agricola called up the reserve troops to fight it out at sword's point. These old soldiers, stabbing with their swords, pushed up the hillside. The Caledonians on the hill-tops came down, but Agricola threw his cavalry against them and ended their advance. The charge became a rout . . . . When the Britons ran into the woods, the general sent the infantry to surround them and to kill them like animals. By nightfall our men had become tired of the killing.'

8 Write three reasons (they are all in this account) to show how Agricola brought about the defeat of the Britons.

Then the march continued. The legions moved into the Highlands, pushing and harassing the Caledonians, while offshore the fleet kept watch. We know from the Roman historian Tacitus that they believed the tribesmen to be rough barbarians. We don't know what the tribes felt, except that they never stopped fighting the soldiers who had invaded their lands.

Deep in the Highlands, the Romans won a great victory. But how were they going to keep control of a territory full of forests, mountains and lakes? They needed a huge army to chase the tribesmen who, after their defeat, disappeared into the forests. As for Agricola, some people in Rome were jealous of his successes. He was told to return to Italy and was never again given the command of an army. In Britain, the legions returned to the line of forts that Agricola had built linking the rivers Forth and Clyde and abandoned the mountains of the far north.

17 Hadrian's Wall

Hadrian's Wall as it is today. About six feet of the top of the Wall has been lost by over 1800 years of fierce weather and by the work of stone robbers

1 Which is the north side of the Wall? Which is the south (Roman) side? How do you know?

2 How did the Romans make full use of the land on which this section of the Wall was built? Write down reasons to explain why this was a good place to build the Wall.

Sketch map of Hadrian's Wall

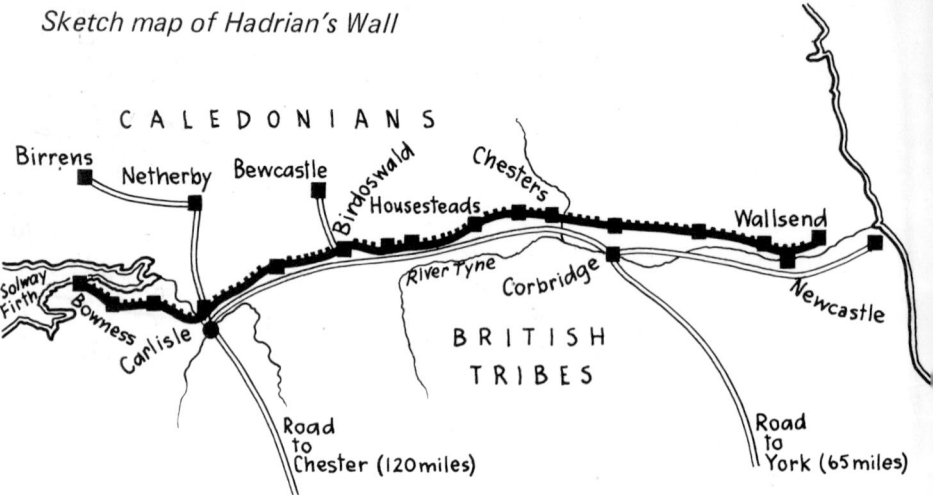

3 Using the evidence of the sketch-map, explain what natural features (rivers, the sea, etc.) helped the Romans.

In the year AD 117, Hadrian became Emperor of Rome. He was told that the Britons could not be kept under control. He went to Britain to see the situation for himself. Standing on the banks of the River Tyne, he looked across the wild countryside to the hills where the northern tribesmen, the Caledonians, lived. Hadrian decided that a wall should be built. It would be a dividing line between the northern tribesmen and the Roman zone to the south. Hadrian returned to Rome, leaving the Governor of Britain to carry on the work. An army of stonemasons, engineers, soldiers and labourers, taken from the British tribes, set to work.

When it was eventually finished, Hadrian's Wall stretched for 80 miles across the narrowest neck of land in northern Britain, from the Solway Firth to the River Tyne.

Where the Wall crossed flat ground, the Romans added to the defences.

An artist's impression of Hadrian's Wall

4 Compare this picture with the one on the opposite side of this Opening. What differences can you see between the Wall in Roman times from the Wall today?

5 What differences do you see between the countryside on the north side of the Wall and on the south (Roman) side?

6 Imagine that you are either *a* a Roman sentry on duty in the turret or *b* a tribesman living here when the Romans came. Write a description of what you would see if you were on the Wall, or approaching it.

7 What do the letters LEG mean? What was the number of this legion? The letters AUG are short for *Augusta*, which means 'the Emperor's Legion'. Find these letters.

8 What animals can you see on the stone which made up the badge of the legion?

A legionary stone. Each legion was responsible for building part of the Wall. When the work was finished, the name and number of the legion was carved on a stone and was set into the Wall

A Roman mystery: what was the *vallum*?

To the north of the Wall a deep ditch was dug, with the earth piled up to make a mound. On the Roman side a road ran parallel with the Wall. This allowed troops to march quickly to where the tribesmen were attacking. Beyond this road, another ditch called the *vallum* was dug. For many years, historians did not understand the purpose of this ditch on the Roman side. It is now thought that it separated the garrison on the Wall from the civilians who lived in the villages to the south.

The men who built the Wall served with the legions. Stone-masons cut the stone from quarries.

Soldiers (helped by British labourers) cleared the ground, laid the stones for the foundations and gradually built up the Wall.

When it was first built, the Wall was 15 feet (4.5 metres) high, and 8 to 10 feet (about 3 metres) wide. There were seventeen forts where most of the soldiers lived. Between the forts were mile-castles and look-out posts called turrets. Roads linked the Wall with the forts at Chester and York.

18 Attack at Hadrian's Wall

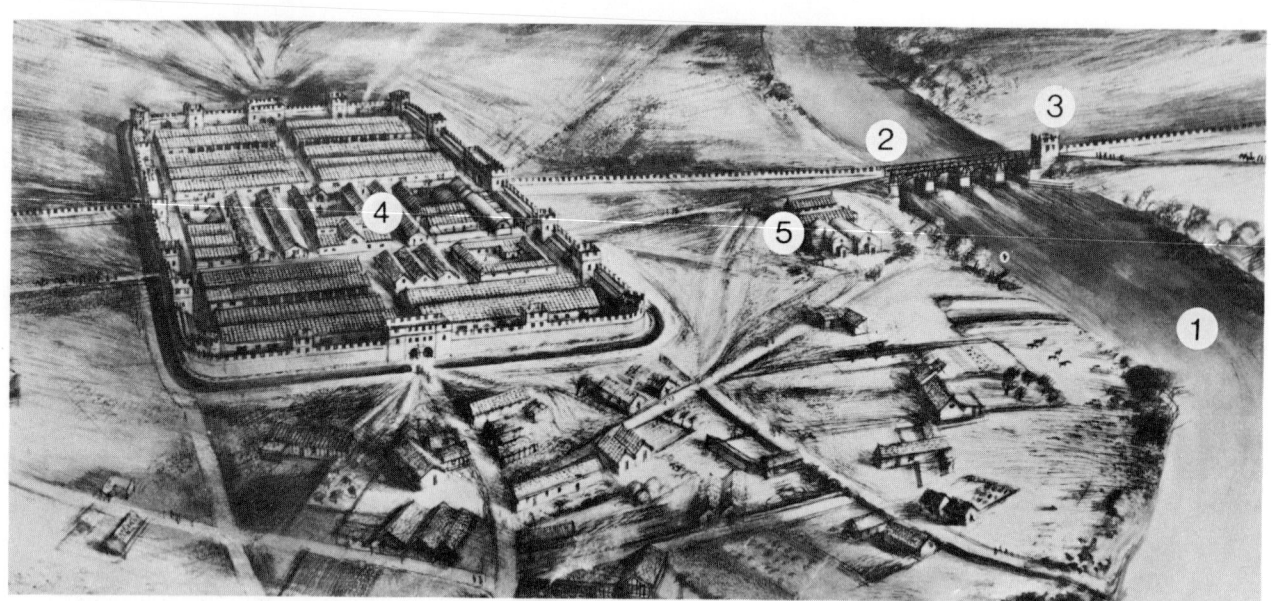

An artist's impression of Chesters fort in about the year AD 180. The garrison that patrolled Hadrian's Wall lived in forts such as the one at Chesters

1 Find the line of the wall and the outer walls of the fort.

2 Where was the village where the soldiers' families lived?

3 Write the numbers 1 to 5 in your book. Against each number write the name of the part of the fort, choosing from the words in the box:

turret	River Tyne
bridge	baths
headquarters	

4 Make a list of the strong points of the fort. Are there any places where the fort could have been strengthened?

5 Make a time-chart to show the main events in the history of Hadrian's Wall from when it was surveyed in AD 117 to when it was finally destroyed (around AD 400-420). Begin with:
117 : the line of the Wall surveyed . . . .

The forts on the Wall

The forts were the strong points along the 73-mile length of the Wall. Some of them, such as Chesters, were built to sit astride the Wall, with gateways to the north of it. Forts were oblong-shaped and each one was laid out to a similar basic pattern. The main street led from the main gate to the centre of the town where the head-quarters building was situated. Long rows of barracks for the soldiers, granaries for the storage of corn and stables for the cavalry horses were built in neat rows within the fort. Some of the big forts could accommodate 1000 men, or 500 cavalrymen and their horses. Outside the walls of the fort was the village, where the wives and families of the soldiers lived, and where there were shops and inns. Chesters had a large bath-house, built very near to the river, for the ordinary soldiers to use.

The Wall was started in AD 122 and completed ten years later. In the following years, life in the forts was usually peaceful. However, on several occasions the Caledonians attacked. They crossed the Wall, breaking through at a turret or a mile-castle.

These tools were found by archaeologists near Hadrian's Wall

6 Draw each tool and write the name (chosen from the box) against each one.

> a spade, a plumb bob, nails, the head of a mason's hammer

7 Imagine that the Wall is under attack by Caledonian tribesmen. Write out these events in the order in which they would happen (1, 2, 3, 4):

> a sentry gives the alarm
>
> troops ride quickly along the road to the danger spot
>
> a fire-signal is set alight
>
> the tribesmen move in to attack

8 Explain why these were important to the defences of the Wall:
   a a mile-castle; *b* a fort; *c* a fire-signal.

9 Suppose that you were leading a Caledonian army. Describe (with drawings) how you would attack the Wall.

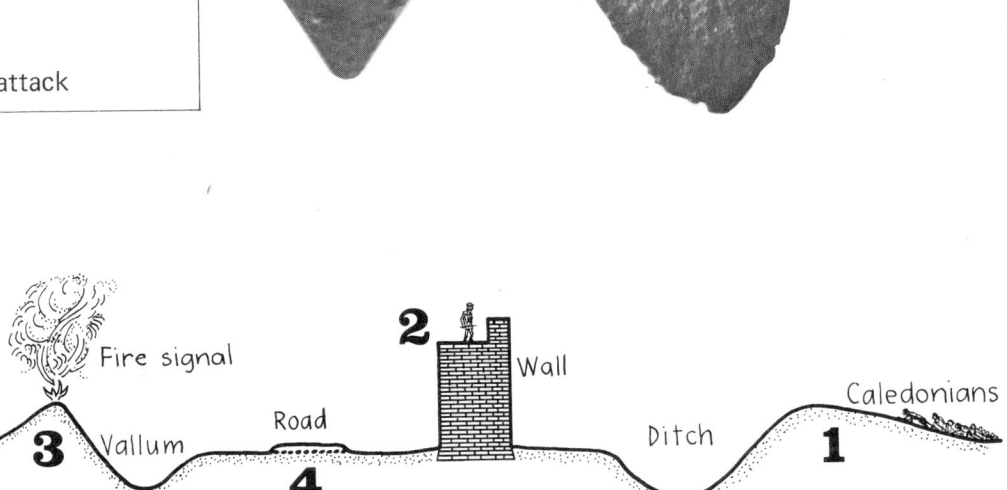

Under attack

When the Caledonian tribesmen crossed the Wall, they were usually after cattle or corn. When the raid was over, they returned to their own camps, far to the north of Hadrian's Wall. In the year AD 196 there was a sudden invasion. The tribes burnt several of the forts and killed many soldiers. It took the Romans over five years to recapture the forts and to repair the damage.

In the year AD 367 the Caledonians joined the Saxon raiders from across the North Sea. Again the Wall was over-run, forts were burned and the Romans had to retreat to York. After they had recovered the lost territories, the Romans moved their families, cattle and valuable goods into the forts. The grain stores and the barracks became the homes of the villagers.

From about the year AD 400, the sea rovers were able to enter Britain quite freely, and the northern tribesmen crossed the Wall whenever they wished. As the Romans retreated into southern Britain, and then finally left for Rome, the Wall fell into decay. The Saxons and Caledonians took away the stone for their own houses; grass and trees grew over the ruins. But the Wall can still be followed today, right across the north of England.

19 The Antonine Wall

A stone slab found at the eastern end of the Antonine Wall. It is believed to date from about AD 143. It is now in the Museum of Antiquities in Edinburgh

1 Explain why it is obvious that the stone was the work of a stone-mason working for the *Roman* army.

2 Explain (with diagrams) how the Antonine Wall was different from Hadrian's Wall.

3 Using the information given below, explain why:
   a the Romans advanced into Scotland
   b they built the Antonine Wall

4 Estimate approximately how far (in miles) the Antonine Wall was from Hadrian's Wall.

The land of the Caledonian tribes

In the year AD 138 Antoninus Pius became Emperor of Rome. He ordered the Governor of Britain to recover the lands once occupied by the Romans in the far north of Britain, but which later had been abandoned.

The Governor advanced north into the territory of the Caledonian tribes. It took the army three years to defeat the tribes. The Governor of Britain therefore decided to build a new wall. It would follow the valleys of the two rivers, Forth and Clyde. The wall would keep the tribesmen penned in the north country.

First, a stone foundation was laid. On top of it was placed a turf wall. The bulk of the digging and building was done by the soldiers of the legions and the auxiliary units, although slave labour (provided by the defeated tribes) was used for the heaviest work. The Antonine Wall, when finished, was much simpler than Hadrian's Wall. The most northerly wall had no large stone forts, no mile-castles or turrets, no *vallum* (ditch) and no military road alongside the wall.

It measured some 14 feet (4.3 metres) wide, and 10 to 12 feet (3.5 metres) high. On the north-facing wall a parapet was added to give protection to sentries, and in front of the wall was a ditch, 12 feet (3.5 metres) deep.

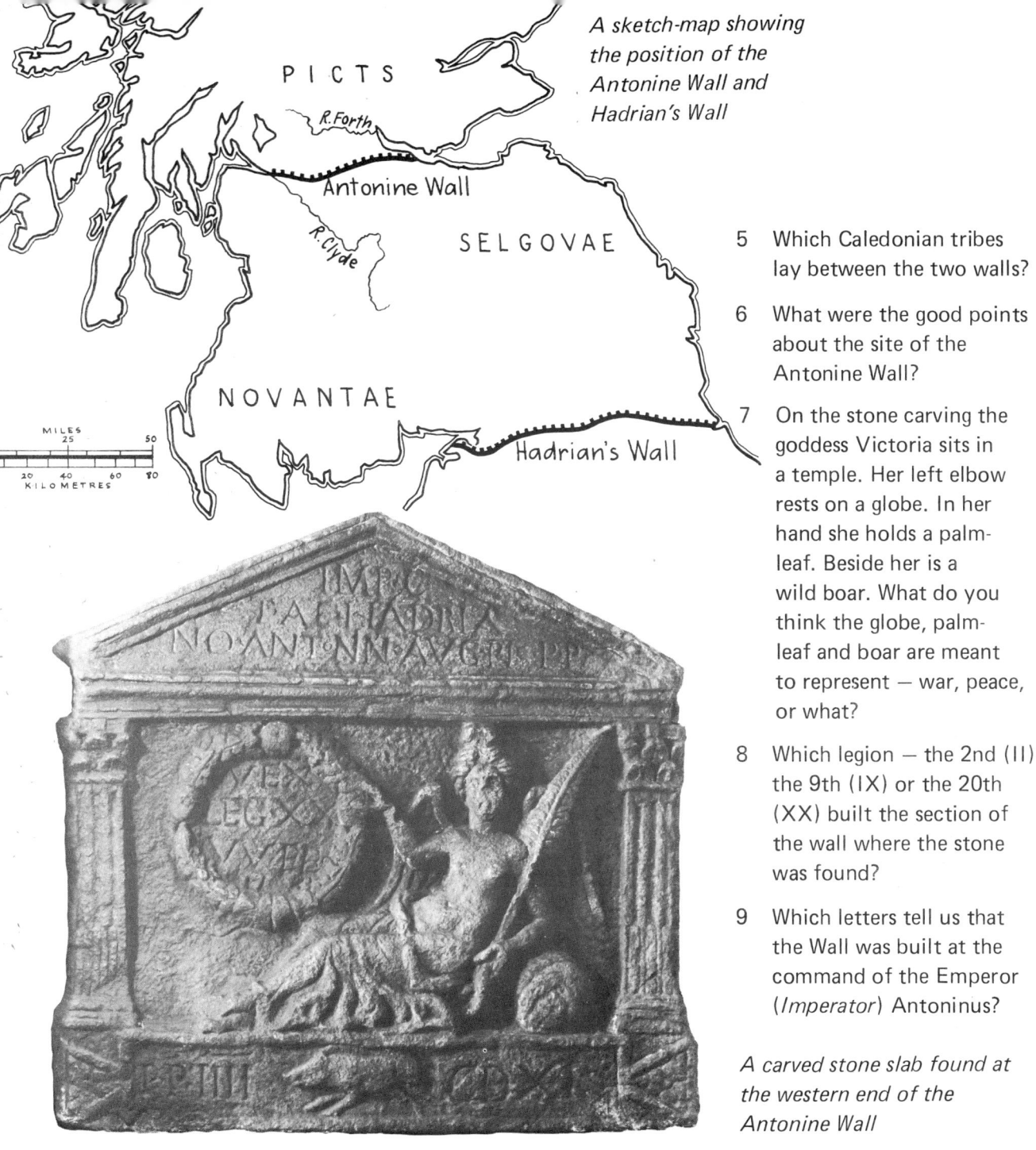

A sketch-map showing the position of the Antonine Wall and Hadrian's Wall

PICTS

R. Forth

Antonine Wall

R. Clyde

SELGOVAE

NOVANTAE

MILES
25 50
20 40 60 80
KILOMETRES

Hadrian's Wall

5 Which Caledonian tribes lay between the two walls?

6 What were the good points about the site of the Antonine Wall?

7 On the stone carving the goddess Victoria sits in a temple. Her left elbow rests on a globe. In her hand she holds a palm-leaf. Beside her is a wild boar. What do you think the globe, palm-leaf and boar are meant to represent — war, peace, or what?

8 Which legion — the 2nd (II), the 9th (IX) or the 20th (XX) built the section of the wall where the stone was found?

9 Which letters tell us that the Wall was built at the command of the Emperor (*Imperator*) Antoninus?

A carved stone slab found at the western end of the Antonine Wall

Along the whole length of the 37-mile wall there were nineteen small turf forts, placed at intervals of about 2 miles. Each fort could take about 400 men. They contained barracks, granaries, store-rooms, stables and the headquarters. At one of these forts, Rough Castle, ten rows of pits were dug. Each pit had a sharpened stake embedded in it, pointing upwards. The whole area of the pits would be covered with branches and grass to make the ground look solid. When the barbarians attacked, they would fall through the branches and on to the stakes.

The retreat to the south

The Antonine Wall was very difficult to hold. In AD 155 two tribes, the Selgovae and the Novantae, attacked and captured some of the forts. Barracks were burned down and the Romans had to retreat. The wall was reoccupied and repaired by the Romans but again, in AD 180, the barbarian tribes proved to be troublesome.

Finally, about the year AD 184, the Romans abandoned the Antonine Wall and retreated to Hadrian's Wall, which again became the most northerly frontier of the Roman Empire. The occupation of Scotland had lasted for only a little more than forty years.

20 Roads

Watling Street — a photograph of a Roman road taken from the air

1 With tracing paper, trace from the photograph the line of this part of Watling Street. Draw a straight line with a ruler along the road. Where does the road deviate from a straight line? Write down reasons to explain why you think the Romans had to vary the road from a straight line.

2 Now look at the cross-section. How wide was the road? How was it drained? Explain why different sizes of stones were used.

A cross-section of a Roman road

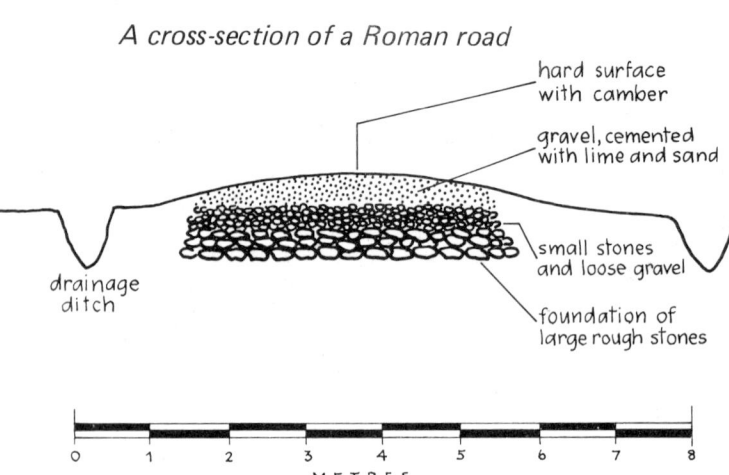

hard surface with camber

gravel, cemented with lime and sand

small stones and loose gravel

foundation of large rough stones

drainage ditch

0 1 2 3 4 5 6 7 8
METRES

Road planning

Archaeologists know of 7500 miles of roads built by the Romans in Britain. No doubt there are hundreds more lying beneath modern towns and country fields.

The roads allowed troops to move quickly to a trouble spot. They enabled goods to be moved between the towns and ports, and they were needed by the messengers, officials and the Imperial Post on which Rome depended.

To assist travellers and traders, the Romans built inns and stables along the main roads at 15- or 20-mile intervals. Tired horses could be changed, and men could eat, wash and rest.

The roads were laid out in a planned network. There were four main types of road:

1 'Main' roads such as Ermine Street which linked the forts and major towns

2 'Minor' roads built by local people linking small villages to the nearest town or fort

3 In towns, where a main road such as Watling Street carried on through the middle of the town, and where minor roads and pathways criss-crossed the town.

4 The ancient Celtic trackways across the hilltops, which were often used by Roman troops to enable them to march quickly deep into enemy territory.

The road at Wheeldale Moor in Yorkshire is over 1800 years old. The top surface has disappeared and there are ruts that the Romans would have repaired

3   Which roads linked these places:
    Lincoln and London
    London and Wroxeter
    Chichester and London
    Exeter and Lincoln

4   How could troops move quickly from London and Caerleon to Hadrian's Wall?

5   Find the line of the road as it crosses Wheeldale Moor. Estimate the height of the road above the level of the fields. Estimate the width of the road. How high was the road above field level in Roman times (see text below)?

6   Make a list of the stages in the building of a Roman road.

7   Write down several reasons to explain why the Romans thought roads were so important.

The main roads and towns of Roman Britain

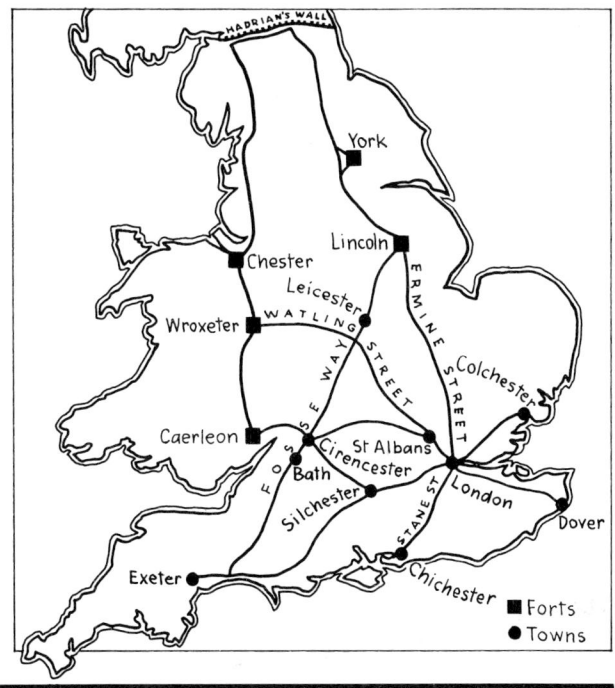

Road building

Engineers from the legions usually took control of the building operations. They walked over the route to survey it. Having decided on the line of the road, and how rivers and hills would be crossed, the work then began. Lighted beacons were used as guidelines. The engineers tried to keep to a straight line but rivers and steep valleys had to be avoided.

The trees, gorse and turf were cleared away. Then a raised embankment was laid down. It consisted of earth taken from two drainage ditches which took all the water running from the road surface.

The earth embankment can now only be seen in air photographs, but in Roman times it stood over a metre above the level of the fields. To hold the large stones, gravel and smaller stones together, the engineers used 'cement' — a mixture of sand, water and lime.

On some of the town roads the Romans placed heavy flagstones on the surface. These are often unearthed in excavations. Place-names also give clues. When the Saxons came, they gave the name 'streat' to describe a Roman road. When this word is used in a town name such as Stratton, Street, Streatham, Staneford, it may mean that there was once a Roman road there.

21 Towns

Right: *A photograph from the air of Silchester as it is today*

1 After the Romans left Silchester, it was not built over. The outline of the buildings can now be seen from the air. In the photograph find the line of the outer ditch, the outer wall, the forum, the public baths, the amphitheatre and a temple.

2 How many gates were there?

3 Make a list of the additions that have been made to the landscape at Silchester since Roman times (a farm, fields, etc.)

4 Explain what went on in these places in Roman times: *a* the *forum* (market-place); *b* a temple; *c* an amphitheatre.

Right: *Diagram showing the lay-out of the Roman town of Silchester in Hampshire*

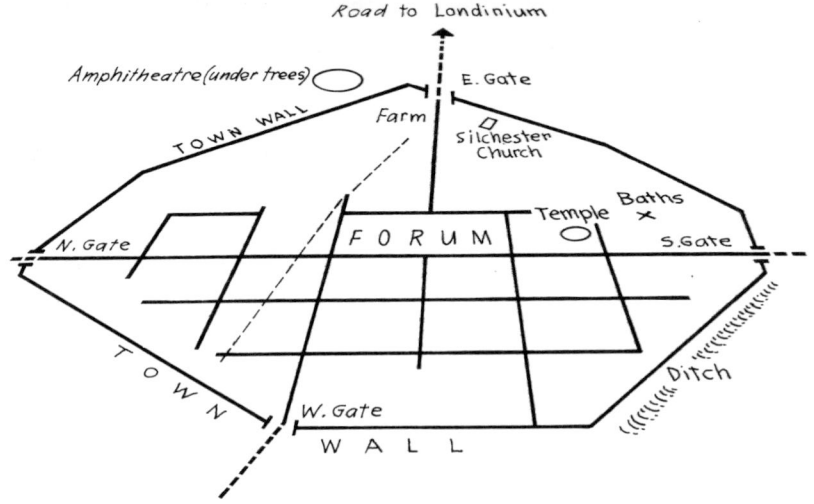

Road to Londinium

Amphitheatre (under trees)

E. Gate

TOWN WALL

Farm

Silchester Church

Temple   Baths x

N. Gate

F O R U M

S. Gate

T O W N

Ditch

W. Gate

W A L L

The new towns of Roman Britain

Before the Romans arrived, the British tribes did not have towns. They lived mostly on farms, and only in time of danger did they come together in a 'capital' — a collection of huts surrounded by a ditch. The Romans introduced many changes. First, they built the forts, then the roads, and lastly the towns. Most of the towns were in southern Britain. The first was built in AD 49. A town for retired soldiers called a *colonia* was started at Colchester. Not far away the town of Verulamium (St Albans) was built. This had been the main settlement of the Catuvellauni tribe. The town, burned down in AD 60 by Boudicca's tribesmen, was later rebuilt.

In later years London became the financial and administrative centre and by far the largest town in Britain. Three other *colonia* for veteran soldiers were built at Gloucester, York and Lincoln. Governor Agricola carried on the work by sending surveyors, architects and stonemasons to assist the tribal leaders to extend their capitals. Among the fourteen towns known to us was Calleva Atrebatum, now called Silchester, a small village in Hampshire.

An artist's impression of the forum at Verulamium (St Albans) in the second century

5 What is taking place in the forum? The stone column in the centre has a statue at the top. Whose statue do you think this might be?

6 The town council met in a building called the *basilica* (town hall). Find the councillors (in a procession) and the basilica. What would the other large buildings be used for?

7 Here are some town names in Latin. Use a book such as *Life in Roman Britain* by A. Birley or reference books in the library to find out their modern English names: Eboracum, Ratae, Deva, Camulodunum, Verulamium, Corinium.

8 According to Tacitus, what were the attractions for the Britons of having Roman towns?

A 'life of ease'

Tacitus, the Roman historian, wrote that 'towns accustomed the Britons to a life of ease and peace. Often, assistance for the building of temples, squares and houses was given. And so the people were led into the temptations of banquets and baths. But these novelties were only a feature of their slavery.' Agricola believed that the Romans 'civilized' and tamed the rough Britons by making them live in towns. The Romans gave the Britons fine buildings, but they also demanded that taxes be paid. Roman officials passed local laws, and law courts made sure that the Britons obeyed the laws. The houses which the Romans and the richer Britons lived in were long, narrow buildings. Later, houses were often built around an open courtyard. Nearby would be bath-houses, and perhaps there would be a theatre, as at Silchester and St Albans.

When the Romans left Britain, the towns were looted and burned by the Saxons. Farmers took away the stone for cow byres and farmsteads. Grass and trees grew in the once busy streets.

The sites of Roman towns such as York, Dorchester and Exeter were often used again, centuries later, for medieval towns.

22 Shops

A stone carving of a Roman shop. From a monument in Rome, in the first century AD

1 What kind of shop do you think this is — a butcher's, a shoemaker's or a cutler's (a maker of knives and kitchen utensils)?

2 What do you notice about the clothing worn by the shopkeeper and his customer?

3 What different kinds of tools are on display in the shop? What do you think these tools would be used for?

4 Imagine that you are a Roman shopkeeper or his wife selling fruit and vegetables from a market stall. Write out a list of the things you would have for sale. Draw a poster or a picture to show the stall and what is for sale.

Shopping day

Into the *forum* (the market-place), with its busy stalls, the farmers brought vegetables (peas, beans, cabbages), corn and fruit. They shouted to passers-by to come and buy. In the narrower streets of the town, at the front of narrow little shops, the wives of the shopkeepers displayed the goods for sale. Among the objects sold were shoes, clothing, bread, tools, bowls and pottery, glass bottles, wine, cooking oil and stone carvings such as small statues to decorate the houses.

The craftsmen who made these things worked at the back of the shop. Among them were shoemakers and cobblers, carpenters, locksmiths, blacksmiths, masons and others.

Roman shops were much smaller than those of today. Some towns had no shops at all, only stalls set up on market days. In the bigger towns such as London, the shopkeepers worked from two rooms. The front room was used to display the goods they had for sale. The back room was their workshop where things were made.

At the end of the day the shopkeeper and his wife would board up the shop-front and retire to the back room or to a room upstairs where the rest of the family lived.

An artist's impression of a street scene in London in about AD 200

5 How many different kinds of transport can you find in this picture? Make a list of them.

6 What do you think the shop on the right of the picture is selling?

7 From what materials (bricks, tiles, etc.) are these houses and shops constructed?

8 Imagine that you are a boy or girl of a poor family, living in a town in Roman Britain. Write an account, as if for a page in a diary, of a day in your life.

In the slums

Roman towns also had their slums. The poorest people — labourers, shopkeepers' assistants, wives of soldiers serving in far-off lands, widows and others — lived in wooden shacks. They used the floor for their beds; they ate scraps of food thrown away from the kitchens of wealthier people, and they were very glad to find any kind of labouring job. The rooms they lived in would be gloomy and dirty, small and crowded. In all Roman houses, sewage was primitive. Only Lincoln and York are known to have had underground sewers. Normally, rubbish was thrown into pits and covered with earth when the smell became unbearable. Water came from wells dug outside the town's walls or in the gardens. Not surprisingly, there were regular outbreaks of disease and illnesses which accounted for the high number of deaths in Roman towns.

Wealthier people lived more comfortably. In the town of Wroxeter a house of twenty rooms has been discovered. It had underfloor heating, baths and flush lavatories. The walls of this house were plastered and painted, and some of the floors were covered with colourful mosaics.

23 Farms and villas

This bronze corn measure was found at Carvoran in Northumberland. It dates from about AD 90

1 Every farm, whether owned by a Roman or a Briton, was visited by an official. He collected corn from the farmer. Would this official be *a* a shopkeeper; *b* an army officer; or *c* a tax collector?

2 How do you think the measure was used?

3 It is thought that the measure was used in the reign of one of the emperors (*Caesare*). Whose name is on the measure? Is it: Nero, Trajan, Germanicus?

4 Use the information below to make a list of the *advantages* that the Romans brought to farming in Britain. Write out a second list of the *disadvantages* that arose from the Roman occupation of the land.

5 The name of the Emperor Domitian was scratched out from the measure after his death in AD 96. No one knows why. What do you think might have happened?

Life on the farm

When the Romans invaded Britain, they found a country of farmers. The Britons grew wheat, barley and vegetables, and grazed sheep and cattle. For a time, the Romans let the farmers continue in their old ways, as long as enough corn was produced to feed the army. But as the demand for food grew, the Romans interfered more and more in farming methods. They brought into Britain a larger iron plough which was used to farm heavier ground. They had better hand tools such as scythes (an iron blade used for cutting corn) and spades. But above all the conquerors introduced better business methods. They built roads and towns, making it easier for farmers to take goods to markets some distance away. They arranged for British grain to be sent abroad, and they built airy granaries where corn could be dried and stored over the winter.

As the years passed, the Britons found that the Roman methods worked. More land was cultivated. Corn could be kept longer, and new crops such as apples, cherries and carrots were introduced into Britain.

But there was trouble, too. Officials came to every farm to collect the corn tax by which all farmers had to hand over a part of every crop to the army.

An artist's impression of the Roman villa at Chedworth, in Gloucestershire

6 The numbers on the picture refer to parts of the villa on the right. Write out the number and the part of the villa that you think it refers to.

> guest rooms
> central courtyard
> owner's living area
> farm buildings
> shrine to the god of a spring
> a bath-house

7 What has been done to give the villa some protection from robbers or from an attack?

8 Draw a sketch or a diagram to show how a Roman courtyard villa was planned. Label the different parts of the villa listed in question 6. Add the kitchens, stables and the outer fence.

9 Imagine that you are Marcus or Livilla, the son or daughter of the owner of Chedworth villa. Write an account of your work in the villa, including a visit by friends from Londinium.

In time of war, the army had the right to seize the whole crop. Land was also taken from the Britons. Many retired Roman soldiers were given land once owned by tribes such as the Trinovantes.

The villas

Villas were large estates owned and farmed by the more prosperous Roman and British farmers. The sites of over 600 villas have been found. Ninety per cent of them were in southern Britain. They were built in sheltered valleys or on hillsides where herds of sheep grazed.

The first villas were no more than a long corridor with rooms off it. In larger villas, rooms were added around a central courtyard. Among the buildings in a courtyard villa would be rooms for the owner, baths, kitchens, guest rooms, etc., and stables, cow byres and barns for the work of the farm. In the fourth century, when many farmers turned to sheep rearing, some of the barns were converted into mills.

Most of these villas were small. They had only two or three rooms for the farmer and his family and a slave or two. Chedworth was an exception with its thirty rooms, a temple, baths, gardens and warm-air central heating.

24 A palace fit for a king

An artist's impression of the palace at Fishbourne in the second century AD

Fishbourne is thought to have been the palace of a British ruler in southern Britain, King Cogidubnus. He surrendered to and helped the Romans and was given lands in return. A stone from the palace was found near Fishbourne: it reads:

1   Match the numbers in the picture of the palace to these parts of it: the formal gardens, main hall, guest rooms, harbour, baths.

2   What evidence is there in the picture to show that the palace was owned by a wealthy man?

3   According to the inscription, to which two Roman gods was the temple dedicated? Which guild paid for the temple?

4   A *legate* was an officer who served the emperor. What is there in the name and titles of Cogidubnus to show that he was a friend of the Romans?

'This temple was erected to Neptune and Minerva and for the prosperity of the Imperial Family, by the members of the Metalworkers guild, at their own expense, and under the protection of Tiberius Claudius Cogidubnus, King and Imperial Legate in Britain. The palace was given by Clemens, son of Pudentinus.'

During the invasion of Britain in AD 43, a section of the Roman army advanced into what is now the county of Sussex. The British ruler was a man called Cogidubnus. He gave in to the Romans. In return for his help, he was given lands and power. As a local governor he called himself 'king' and was given Roman titles.

A ruined palace
In 1960, a workman who was digging the foundations of a watermain in the village of Fishbourne came across a mass of old rubble. He told the engineer, who reported it to the local archaeological group. When more stone buildings were found, along with pottery and other material, it was decided to start a big 'dig'. After eight years of excavations by archaeologists, the foundations of a large palace were laid bare. Was this the home of 'King' Cogidubnus, friend and ally of the Roman conquerors?

As the place was excavated, it became obvious that whoever had owned it had been rich and powerful. Around a central garden were arranged the four wings of a large palace. Behind the building another garden ran down to the sea. To the west of the building were stables, servants' quarters and store-rooms.

In the four wings of the main palace were large

A mosaic of a boy riding a dolphin, found in the north wing of the palace at Fishbourne

5 Describe each of the beasts shown in the mosaic. Draw some of the designs on this mosaic.

6 After looking at pictures of several other Roman mosiacs (to be found in illustrated library books on the Romans), draw a mosaic floor of your own design.

7 Describe in your own words how a mosaic was made by a Roman craftsman.

8 Explain why you think Fishbourne may (or may not) have been the palace of Cogidubnus.

rooms — dining rooms, bedrooms and living rooms for the owner and his family. There were separate apartments for visitors. All the rooms in the owner's area had mosaic floors, walls that had been plastered and painted, and underfloor heating. To the rear of the palace was a kitchen garden. Beside it was a bread oven large enough to make bread for hundreds of people. Walled gardens, baths, banqueting rooms, central heating — this was how a great ruler lived in Roman Britain. But was it Cogidubnus?

Beautiful objects — but no names

The excavations at Fishbourne led to the discovery of bones, pottery, knives, toys, tiles and pins. But among all this material there was nothing with Cogidubnus' name on it — so the mystery is unsolved.

Amongst the rubble there were many mosaics from the mosaic floors that were so popular.

Mosaics were made by fitting small pieces of brick, stone and tile on to a 'cement' base. The mosaics were sometimes in the form of a geometrical design, and they often showed magical and real animals, gods or the seasons of the year.

25 Baths and theatres

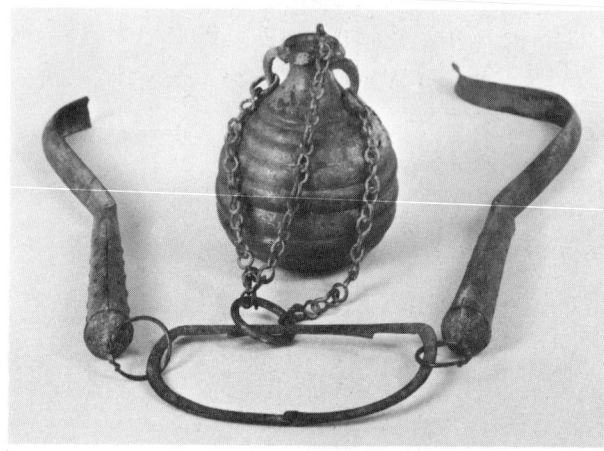

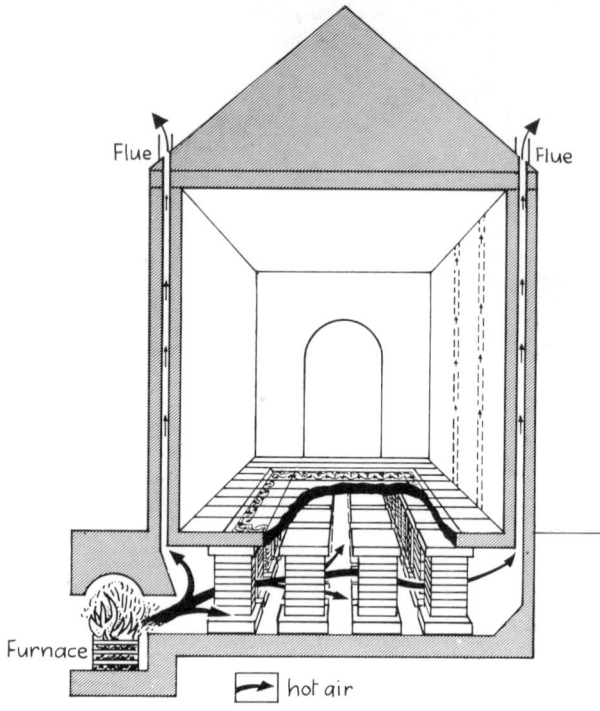

A bather's oil flask and two strigils

1   What did the flask in the picture hold? How do you think a Roman bather used a strigil?

2   In the hypocaust system, follow the arrows and work out how the hot air circulated. Which parts of the room would be the warmest?

3   Draw a picture of the interior of a hot room in a Roman bathhouse. A slave will be using a strigil to clean his master's skin, and other men will be playing dice, enjoying a drink of wine, and talking.

4   In Roman Britain there were no swimming baths except at special places such as Aquae Sulis (Bath). Find out from books on Roman Britain (such as the *Guidebook* for Bath) why people went there in the second and third centuries and what was provided for them there.

The hypocaust. Air was heated by a furnace fuelled with wood, and passed underneath the floor and through channels (called flues) in the walls

Taking a bath

After a day on the march or in an office, the Romans enjoyed relaxing in a bath. But a Roman bath was quite different from a modern one. Bath-houses were large, with several rooms. At Wroxeter the baths were at the very centre of the town, and at Chesters Fort on Hadrian's Wall a special bath-house was built near to the river for the use of the garrison.

First, the bather exercised in a yard, where he could run, jump, or play a ball game. He then removed his clothes in an outer room and walked into an unheated room to plunge into a cold bath. From there he went into a room where heated air circulated. The floor was supported on stone pillars and hot air and smoke from a furnace travelled through the empty spaces and flues built into the walls. The bather sweated freely and moved on into a very hot room. The Romans did not have soap. Instead they used oil which they carried in a flask. They rubbed the oil into the skin and, using the strigil pictured above, wiped the oil, sweat and dirt from the skin. Then the bather moved into another hot room for a bath. Finally came a cold bath or shower, and the return to the dressing room.

Right: *A pottery jar found at Colchester. It dates from about AD 200 and shows gladiators fighting*

5 What are the two gladiators armed with? Which man do you think will win?

6 On a large sheet of paper, design a poster, with drawings, announcing the contests in the local amphitheatre.

7 In the St Albans theatre, find: *a* the arena; *b* the spectator area; *c* the stage. Draw a sketch-map of the theatre, labelling the parts.

Left: *An aerial photograph of the theatre at St Albans*

Games and good sport

Apart from the baths, there was some public entertainment in Roman times. Theatres were built in several towns. Plays, mimes, dancing and singing took place in these theatres. Much more popular, however, were the performances in the amphitheatres and the chariot hippodromes. At Lincoln, for example, there were chariot races between teams of young men. Professional gladiators came from Rome and Gaul to fight for money or for their freedom in front of crowds of about 4000 or more spectators. One traditional fight was between a gladiator armed with net and trident, and another carrying a shield and sword.

A glass cup found at Colchester shows four gladiators fighting, and gives their names.

For variety, there would be bear-baiting, bull-baiting, wrestling, boxing and foot races, often with bets on the contests. However it is thought that there were no fights between gladiators and animals, such as those performed in the Colosseum in Rome.

26 The gods

A stone slab which was set up by Titus Domitius Cosconianus, a Roman soldier. The stone was an offering to a goddess, Covventina. It is now in the museum at Chesters near to Hadrian's Wall

1 Write down the name of the goddess.

2 The stone slab was found beside a river pool. From the way that the goddess is watching over the pool, would you say she was:
   a a water goddess
   b the protector of Hadrian's Wall
   c some other kind of goddess

3 Write down the full name of the Roman who set up the stone.

4 Draw a picture of the goddess. By examining the slab very closely, you should be able to make your drawing accurate in detail.

5 At the river pool where this stone slab was found, archaeologists also discovered a hoard of 16,000 small coins. What does this 'find' suggest to you about the river pool and the reason why Roman soldiers visited it? Write your reason in your book.

6 Read the text below and books in the library on Celtic gods and the Druids. (One useful book is *Everyday Life of the Pagan Celts* by A. Ross.) Write out a list of names of their gods, and add a sentence explaining why the Romans killed the Druids.

The gods of rivers and sky

The Britons worshipped gods of the sky, the sea, rivers, the sun and moon, the woods and the hills. These gods were carved in stone and wood and were often made to look fierce and terrifying.

The Romans had several different kinds of religion. The most important religion was the worship of the emperor. Temples, altars and statues were set up dedicated to emperors such as Augustus, Hadrian and Trajan. A large temple dedicated to the Emperor Claudius was built at Colchester. It was burned down by the tribesmen of Queen Boudicca in the rising of AD 60.

A second group were the old gods of Rome. Among these were Jupiter, the king of the gods; Juno, his wife; Mars, the god of war; Neptune, the sea-god; Diana, the huntress; Venus, the goddess of love and beauty. These were all worshipped by the Romans who came to Britain. The legions carried statues of them and set up altars and temples to their worship. Each year the commander of a legion or a fort set up a new altar to Jupiter and buried the old altar. Many of these stones have been found by archaeologists.

A temple dedicated to Mithras was found in London. In this picture the artist has imagined Roman soldiers worshipping in the temple, which dates from about AD 200

7 How many priests are there wearing masks of
   a a raven
   b a lion

8 Where is the main altar? Find two stalls with a man in each representing the forces of Light and Darkness.

9 From the evidence of the picture, write down two reasons why the Christians would hate the worship of Mithras.

10 Find out from books in the library (such as *Life in Roman Britain* by A. Birley) the names of some Roman gods. Write out a list of the names of the gods, explaining what each one represented (such as 'Mars, god of war').

Mithras

A third group of gods was brought from overseas. Soldiers serving in the Roman army came from Egypt, Syria, Spain and other countries. They brought the worship of their homeland gods with them. Soldiers from Persia worshipped the god Mithras. He was the God of Good who fought against Evil. In one story, Mithras captured a wild bull. A raven, a messenger from the sun, told Mithras to kill the bull. From its blood came the seeds of life for plants, animals and men. But the creatures of darkness (the dog and the serpent) tried to poison the blood. Mithras fought and defeated these forces of Evil.

The Christians

The Christian religion came to Britain about the year AD 250. For a long time the Christians had to worship in secret. In the fourth century, when the Emperor Constantine became a Christian, the new religion came out into the open.

Archaeologists have found ruined villas with wall plasters carrying the sign of the fish, and an X over a P — both Christian signs. There are a few tombstones with the Latin words *Vivas in Deo* ('May you live in God'). When the Romans left Britain, Christianity was forgotten for many years, until missionaries came to Britain to convert the people again.

27 Growing up

Above: *A stone sculpture showing a boy arriving late for school*

Below: *Writing instruments used by pupils in Roman times*

1　Of the four people in the stone carving, which one is the teacher?

2　What are the two seated boys doing? The boy on the right is late. Roman discipline was strict. What do you think his punishment would be?

3　Write down the numbers 1, 2, 3, 4. Beside them write the names of the writing instruments shown in the picture:

> two metal pens
> a bone pen
> an inkwell
> a wax tablet (a wooden board smeared
> 　with wax)

4　Read the text to find out what subjects were studied by Roman boys. Write out a list of these subjects. Write out a second list of what girls were expected to learn.

A school for some

The early years of a boy's or a girl's life were spent with the family. Then, at the age of six, boys of rich families had a private tutor to teach reading and writing. Later on, they studied mathematics, Greek and Latin. There were schools in most of the big towns. They opened soon after daybreak with one master for about twenty boys. Discipline was strict and boys were beaten for careless work. At the age of twelve, they moved on to more difficult studies. They also had to master the skills of running, jumping and handling weapons such as the sword, spear and bow.

Girls did not go to school. They learned cooking from their mothers. They knew how to run a house and how to spin and weave. It was expected that girls would get married about the age of fourteen or fifteen. Some months before a wedding there was a ceremony where the two families exchanged gifts. The bride's father paid for the wedding, which was usually held in the man's home and not in a church or temple. Families were not large because of the high number of deaths among young children. People died earlier than they do now: thirty-five years was the average length of life.

A *A stone carving showing a tradesman*

B *A stone carving showing a Roman woman having her hair dressed*

1 *a comb* 3 *a nail cleaner*
2 *tweezers* 4 *a necklace*

C *Jewellery and other objects found by archaeologists*

5 In Picture A would you say the man is a: baker, a tailor, or a butcher?

6 In Picture B, which lady is the mistress of the house?

7 Draw pictures of the objects shown in Picture C. Label each drawing.

8 Read the text below. Would you say the man in Picture A is wearing a toga, a stola, or a tunic?

9 Read the text. Would you say the mistress in Picture B is wearing a stola, or a toga?

10 After reading the full text, draw Roman men and women to show how they dressed *a* for cold weather; *b* for an evening meal with guests.

What the Romans wore

Fashion changed very little in the 400 years that the Romans lived in Britain. Most of the time men wore a *tunic*, a loose garment tied at the waist with a belt. Outside, people put on a cloak to keep out the cold. Inside the house, both men and women had sandals with criss-crossing laces. But on muddy roads they wore leather boots with thick soles.

For special occasions, every well-dressed Roman had a *toga*. This was a large and heavy woollen blanket, usually white but sometimes dyed, which was wound around the body. Ladies wore a *stola*, a long dress with sleeves. On colder days, men and women added woollen under-clothes, including a shirt that reached to the knees or ankles. Roman women did not show off their bodies: a glimpse of the ankles was thought to be very daring.

Poorer people had to make do with rougher clothing. Peasants wore a thick woollen tunic. Trousers were strapped to the legs with strips of leather and heavy shoes studded with nails protected their feet.

Both men and women wore brooches, medallions, bracelets and rings. They did not have buttons or buttonholes and so brooches and pins were used to hold their clothing together.

28 At home

The tombstone of Regina, found at the fort of Arbeia (South Shields), a port at the mouth of the River Tyne, near to Hadrian's Wall

1　What was the lady's name? What was her husband's name (on the second line)?

2　What was the Roman name for the fort at South Shields?

3　Barates set up this tombstone when his wife died. How old was she when she died? *An* means 'years', and is followed by the Roman 'XXX'.

4　At Regina's left foot is a work-basket with balls of wool peeping out. On her right is a jewel case. Would you say from the evidence that Barates must have been successful or an unsuccessful merchant?

5　The inscription tells us that Regina came from the Catuvellauni tribe, and that she was once a slave. In what part of Britain did the Catuvellauni live? (The map on Opening 12 will help you.) Draw a sketch-map to show the routes taken by Regina when she travelled north from her home town (suppose it was St Albans) to Arbeia.

Sitting and sleeping

In the towns of Roman Britain, the rich merchants lived comfortably in villas and fine houses. For every wealthy family, there would be twenty or more poor families. We know very little about the poor, because they left very few possessions. The museums of Britain contain many objects made from glass, stone and bronze that give clues to the way of life of rich people who lived in Roman times.

In big houses there would be as many as twelve rooms, including baths and guest rooms. The floors of the dining room and some other main rooms might be made of mosaic; the walls would be painted in bright colours, and warm air would circulate underneath the floors.

Meals were served on low tables, and the family lay on low couches to eat. Beds were wooden frames, with criss-crossing straps of cloth or leather. Sometimes a mattress with blankets and pillows would be placed on the floor of a bedroom.

The Romans sat on wooden seats or cane chairs. Light came from open windows. After dark, the shutters were closed to keep out the night air. Only the very rich could afford glass windows. Lamps or candles had to be lit after dark, so the Romans often went to bed early.

These dishes from a Roman table were found in the city of Camulodunum and are now in the Essex and Colchester Museum

6 Using the picture, make a list of the different kinds of food and drink that the Romans enjoyed.

7 Make a list of the different kinds of bowls and bottles in the picture (a wine glass, a fruit bowl, etc.).

8 What do you think the two pins were used for? Write a sentence to explain how you think they would be used.

9 Read the text below. What would be eaten at a Roman breakfast and banquet? Write out menus for these two meals.

Eating and drinking

Most days started with a light breakfast of bread and fruit. In winter they had a corn mash, rather like porridge. They did not know about tea or coffee, and instead they drank water or wine. At midday, they had another light meal of eggs or fish, with some vegetables and bread. Wine was mixed with water to make it go further.

At an evening banquet there might be seven courses, but on normal days the Romans had one or two courses, followed by fruit. A banquet would begin with eggs or shellfish (oysters were popular in Britain). Then came the meat dish — roast boar, veal, venison, mutton or beef. After the meat they ate puddings, pastries, cakes, fresh or dried fruit, and wine.

To eat their food, the Romans used spoons, knives or fingers. Forks were unknown. They cleaned their teeth with toothpicks. In the kitchen there would be all kinds of bronze and wooden utensils for the cook — spoons, knives, ladles, scales. The Romans were fond of glossy red pottery of the kind shown in the picture, although the Britons made their own pottery from grey clay. Glass bottles and glass cups were used for wine.

29 Invaders from the north

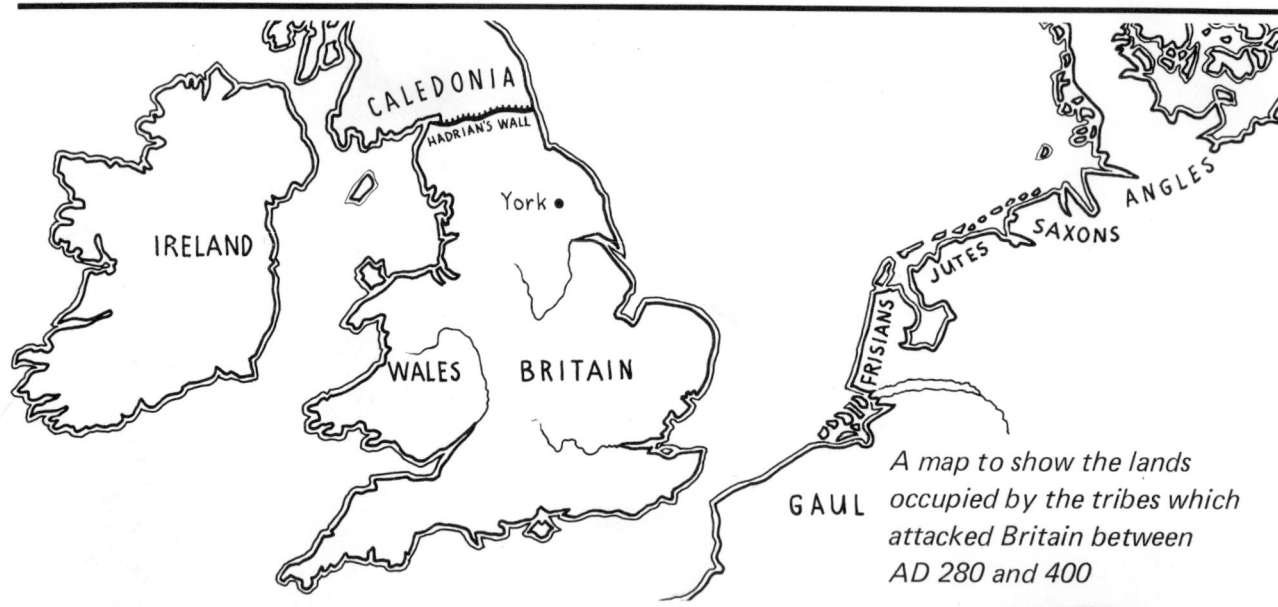

A map to show the lands occupied by the tribes which attacked Britain between AD 280 and 400

1   Copy the map into your notebook. In addition, draw arrows to show the routes that you think would have been taken by the tribes which attacked Britain: *a* Angles and Saxons; *b* Irish; *c* Caledonians (who crossed Hadrian's Wall and advanced to York). Use a different coloured pencil to show each tribe's movements.

2   After reading the information below, write down a list of reasons to explain why the barbarian tribes attacked Britain. Describe what the Romans did to defend themselves.

3   On the medallion, what letters are used to name London?

4   What do the raised arms of the people of London (on the right) show about their feelings towards the general? Who is this general who came to their rescue?

A medallion showing a Roman general called Constantius Chlorus entering London in triumph. The words say 'Restorer of the Eternal Light'

The Romans under attack

Two hundred years after the Roman conquest, a new and dangerous threat arose to Roman Britain. The enemy came from northern Germany, a land of forests beyond the Roman frontier of the River Rhine. At first, these Angles and Saxons came as pirates. They slipped across the North Sea in their long, narrow ships to rob, burn and kill. Just as quickly, they disappeared before extra troops could be sent to deal with them.

To counter these attacks, the Romans built a line of forts along the east coast. These 'forts of the Saxon Shore' with their thick walls gave protection to soldiers, and also provided bases from which ships could set sail to attack the Saxons. In spite of all these defences, more and more raiders crossed the North Sea. To make things worse, the tribes of Caledonia and Ireland grew more daring and harassed the garrisons on Hadrian's Wall and along the Welsh coast.

The Romans were forced to take extra precautions. A special fleet was built to protect Roman merchant shipping and a new commander, the Duke of Britain, set up his headquarters at York.

The eight-sided lighthouse built by the Romans at Dover in Kent

5   The lighthouse was built on a site that commanded good views. Which of these sites do you think the Romans chose:
    a at the entrance to the harbour
    b in the town
    c on the clifftop above the harbour

6   Why do you think the lighthouse was built with eight sides? Write out your explanation.

7   What were the two main purposes of the lighthouse at the time of the Saxon attacks? (The information below will help you.)

8   Match the numbers written on the lighthouse to the uses you think most likely:
    barracks and storeroom
    a beacon to guide ships into harbour
    entrance floor
    the commander's look-out

9   Draw a picture of the lighthouse as it might have looked in Roman times.

10 Find Dover on a map of Britain. Why was Dover a good place to build a lighthouse?

The sea rovers arrive

Another major problem for the Romans was that some of their own troops were not loyal. Some of the Roman generals set themselves up as 'rulers of Britain' and refused to obey orders from Rome. The admiral of the new navy, a man called Carausius, fell into the habit of keeping all of the plunder that he recovered from the Saxon and Angle pirate ships. He was outlawed by the Roman government, but he collected his own army and announced that he was the new 'Emperor of Britain'. In AD 293 Carausius was betrayed and murdered by one of his own men. In AD 296 a Roman general, Constantius Chlorus, crossed from Gaul and restored order in Britain.

Later on, the legions came from Gaul and restored order. But during all this time the unrest and raids had continued, and Hadrian's Wall was crossed by the Caledonians repeatedly.

In the fourth century the attacks grew worse. The Scottish tribes (called the Picts) swept across Hadrian's Wall in AD 310 and advanced to York.

The Roman army tried a new tactic. The invaders were paid in gold and silver if they promised to return home and not to attack the Roman part of Britain.

30 The end of Roman Britain

A photograph from the air of the Roman fort at Richborough, several miles from Dover, in Kent

1 Find these features of the fort:
   a the foundation (the base) of a monument in the shape of a cross, thought to have been built around AD 85.
   b on three sides, the ditches and earth banks of a look-out post built about AD 250.
   c the outer ditches and banks of the Saxon Shore fort, built about AD 320

2 What other foundations can you see? Make an attempt to explain their purpose.

3 Using an atlas, draw a map of southern Britain. Then find and mark on your map these Saxon Shore forts: Carisbrooke, Porchester, Pevensey, Lympne, Dover, Richborough, Reculver, Bradwell, Walton Castle, Burgh Castle.

4 Explain why the Romans built signal stations along the east coast of Britain.

The last years of Roman Britain

The retreat of the Roman legions from Britain began around AD 310. Soldiers were needed to defend other parts of the Empire. As the years passed, the raids by the Saxons, Angles and other northern barbarians increased. Some of these raiders settled in eastern Britain, setting up camps and even farming the land.

In AD 367 the Picts and the Saxons formed an alliance and made a combined attack on the Roman forts. Both the Count of the Saxon Shore and the Duke of Britain (the two leading Roman generals) were killed in the fighting. The Roman Emperor sent a famous general

called Count Theodosius to deal with the grave situation. When he landed, he found London besieged and Kent terrorized by bands of barbarian raiders. He reorganized the army, drove off the pirates and restored order.

In Yorkshire, signal stations were built along the coast to give warning of the approach of enemy ships; the forts at York, Colchester and other places were strengthened; the garrison on Hadrian's Wall was increased, and other precautions were taken. But it was all in vain; nothing could stop the constant Saxon attacks on Britain.

A stone carving from Constantine's Arch in Rome of a cavalry charge into battle

5 In the stone carving find the following:
   legionary standard
   shields (how many?)
   helmets (how many different kinds?)

6 How does the costume of the Roman cavalry differ from their enemy's?

7 Explain (with drawings) how the *ballista* worked and how it could be used in an attack on a castle or walled town.

8 Draw a time-chart from 55 BC to AD 410 to show the main events in the Roman occupation of Britain.

9 Write out a list of reasons to explain why the Romans were forced to retreat from Britain.

A drawing by a modern artist of a Roman catapult called a ballista

The final collapse

In the last years of the fourth century, there were again mutinies in the Roman army. In AD 383 General Maximus took troops from Britain to Gaul in an attempt to seize power. Taking advantage of the Roman weakness, the Picts crossed Hadrian's Wall. The attack was a turning point, for the Wall was never completely recovered and never again fully manned. Many forts were left in ruins.

By the year AD 410 the Romans were seriously worried about the Saxon raids inland, up and down the coast. Meanwhile, attacks on the city of Rome forced the emperor to recall the legions from Britain. In AD 410 Emperor Honorius made a last desperate appeal for troops to return to Italy to defend Rome. Shortly before the city fell, he sent a message telling the provinces to make their own arrangements for defence.

We know little about what happened in Britain. The Saxons and other tribes had a free hand. They brought their families from Germany and settled down. Among the legends is the story of one of the last British leaders, Artorius (known to us as King Arthur), who may have fought the Saxons from his fortress in the West Country.

Acknowledgements

The author and publisher are grateful to the following for their permission to reproduce illustrations:

1 aerial: Cambridge University Collection: copyright reserved; stone: Museum of Antiquities; pots: Lincolnshire City and County Museum/Photo Precision Ltd

2 dinosaur: Reproduced by courtesy of the Trustees of the British Museum (Natural History)

3 bison: Mansell Collection; horse: © Archives Photgraphiques Paris/SPADEM

4 burial mound: Crown Copyright: reproduced by permission of the Controller of Her Majesty's Stationery Office; weaponheads: Lincolnshire City and County Museum/Photo Precision Ltd; pots: Reproduced by courtesy of the Trustees of the British Museum; hut: Crown Copyright: reproduced by permission of the Department of the Environment

5 aerial: Aerofilms Ltd

6 aerial: Aerofilms Ltd; cauldron and trumpet: Reproduced by courtesy of the Trustees of the British Museum; reconstruction: Crown Copyright: reproduced by permission of the Controller of Her Majesty's Stationery Office

7 4 articles: Reproduced by courtesy of the Trustees of the British Museum; farm: Crown Copyright reserved/COI

8 chariot: National Museum of Wales; coins: Ashmolean Museum, Oxford; sword: Reproduced by courtesy of the Trustees of the British Museum

9 aerial: Aerofilms Ltd; fort: Crown Copyright: reproduced by permission of the Department of the Environment

10 coins: Reproduced by courtesy of the Trustees of the British Museum; ditch: G. Tingay

11 statue: Radio Times Hulton Picture Library; stone carving: Mansell Collection

12 skeleton: Society of Antiquaries of London; shields: Grosvenor Museum, Chester City Council

13 tombstone: Colchester and Essex Museum

14 left: Colchester and Essex Museum; right: Gloucester City Museum and Art Gallery

15 aerial: Cambridge University Collection: copyright reserved; reconstruction: National Museum of Wales

16 mould: Trustees of the Corbridge Excavation Fund, photographer Terry Hay; aerial: Cambridge University Collection: copyright reserved

17 photo and reconstruction: Crown Copyright: reproduced by permission of the Controller of Her Majesty's Stationery Office; legionary stone: Philipson Studios, Newcastle upon Tyne

18 all photos: Crown Copyright: reproduced by permission of the Controller of Her Majesty's Stationery Office

19 left: National Museum of Antiquities of Scotland; right: Hunterian Museum, Glasgow

20 aerial: Cambridge University Collection: copyright reserved; road: British Tourist Authority

21 aerial: Cambridge University Collection: copyright reserved; reconstruction: copyright reserved: Verulamium Museum, St Albans

22 shop: Mansell Collection; street: The Museum of London

23 corn measure: Trustees of the Clayton Collection (Chesters Museum), photographer Terry Hay; reconstruction: The National Trust

24 left and right: Sussex Archaeological Trust

25 implements: Reproduced by courtesy of the Trustees of the British Museum; jar: Colchester and Essex Museum aerial: Aerofilms Ltd

26 stone: Trustees of the Clayton Collection (Chesters Museum), photographer Terry Hay; temple: The Museum of London

27 stone carvings: Mansell Collection; writing instruments and C 1-3: The Museum of London; C4: Reproduced by courtesy of the Trustees of the British Museum

28 tombstone: South Tyneside Central Library; dishes: Colchester and Essex Museum

29 medallion: Cambridge University Library; lighthouse: Crown Copyright: reproduced by permission of the Controller of Her Majesty's Stationery Office

30 aerial: Crown Copyright: reproduced by permission of the Controller of Her Majesty's Stationery Office; stone carving: Radio Times Hulton Picture Library

All drawings by Malcolm Booker